the powerfood
cookbook

Rachael Anne Hill & Tamsin Burnett-Hall

the powerfood cookbook

great recipes for high energy and healthy weight-loss

RYLAND
PETERS
& SMALL

LONDON NEW YORK

senior designer   Paul Tilby
senior editors   Julia Charles, Henrietta Heald
production   Patricia Harrington
art director   Anne-Marie Bulat
publishing director   Alison Starling

food stylists   Tamsin Burnett-Hall, Rachel Miles
prop stylist   Clare Macdonald
indexer   Hilary Bird

First published in the USA in 2007
by Ryland Peters & Small, Inc.
519 Broadway
5th Floor
New York, NY 10012
www.rylandpeters.com

10 9 8 7 6 5 4 3 2 1

ISBN-13: 978-1-84597-375-9
ISBN-10: 1-84597-375-5

A CIP record for this book
is available from the Library of Congress.

Printed and bound in China.

Notes

Uncooked or partially cooked eggs should not be served
to very old or frail people, very young children, pregnant
women, or people with a compromised immune system.

All fruits and vegetables should be washed thoroughly and
peeled, unless otherwise stated. Unwaxed citrus fruits
should be used whenever possible.

Every effort has been made by the authors and the publisher
to ensure that the information given in this book is complete
and accurate. This book is not intended as a substitute for
proper medical advice. Always consult your doctor on matters
regarding health. Neither the authors nor the publisher shall
be held responsible for any loss, injury, or damage allegedly
arising from any information or suggestion in this book.

contents

introduction

powerfoods and why we need them

This book is all about putting back the "power" into the food we eat. It is also about the power we have to control our weight, to prevent major lifestyle diseases, to stay fit and healthy, and, most of all, to boost our energy levels.

Too often, we wake up feeling tired and push ourselves through our daily chores before collapsing in front of the television for the evening. This book aims to show how, with a few small alterations to normal eating habits and the inclusion of a whole variety of vitamin-and-mineral-packed "powerfoods," it is possible to change all that. Here are three simple steps to power eating:

STEP 1: TAKE CONTROL OF WHAT YOU EAT

It is no surprise that, in doctors' consulting rooms across the land, the most common complaint is tiredness. The reason is twofold. The vast majority of the foods we have grown used to eating are so overprocessed that they release their sugars too quickly into the bloodstream, giving us a short-lived energy "high" followed by a fatigue- and hunger-inducing "low." Many foods are also stripped of their natural goodness, leaving us deficient in vital nutrients.

In the name of convenience, we have come to rely on factory workers to prepare our food for us. Even people who profess to enjoy cooking may be surprised about the amount of pre-prepared and processed foods they eat, if they consider it seriously. After all, a large proportion of the foods we routinely eat, such as breakfast cereal, health-food bars, yogurts, pre-prepared meals, cooking sauces, drinks, sandwiches, and desserts, are manufactured by others. There is nothing wrong with that if they are consumed in moderation, but it is when we begin to rely almost entirely on other people to make our food for us, that problems with our health, waistline, and energy levels begin.

Despite the millions of dollars spent by food manufacturers to convince us of the virtue of their products, their primary aim is to make money, not to look after our health—and no one knows better than the food industry that the three key ingredients guaranteed to get our taste buds tingling and our hands reaching into our pockets to buy more are fat, salt, and sugar!

That is why the most effective thing you can do to improve your diet is to get back into the kitchen. In doing so, you will not only be cutting out the need for all those additives and preservatives required to enable a food to sit on a supermarket shelf, but, because you are cooking fresh foods from scratch, you will also significantly increase your intake of immune-boosting and disease-preventing vitamins, minerals, and antioxidants.

STEP 2: BASE YOUR MEALS ON POWERFOODS

All the recipes included in this book are based on powerfoods. These are foods that pack a powerful nutritional punch, such as fruit, vegetables, fish, nuts, seeds, beans, and good-quality lean meats. They are not only rich in essential vitamins, minerals, antioxidants, and fiber, but they release their energy in a slow, steady fashion, helping to avoid dramatic sugar highs and lows, leaving us feeling energized and sustained all day long.

STEP 3: GO FOR FOODS WITH A LOW GI/GL RATING

Powerfoods also generally rate low on the glycemic index (GI), a term that is explained in full on the following pages, along with glycemic load (GL). The index was devised by scientists investigating the speed at which various forms of carbohydrate release their sugars into the bloodstream.

Until recently, carbohydrates were divided into two categories: simple and complex. Simple carbohydrates were the sugary types, such as those in honey, jelly, candy, cakes, chocolate, and cookies. Complex carbohydrates included potatoes, rice, pasta, bread, and cereals. It was thought that simple carbohydrates caused our blood sugar level to rise far more rapidly and give us a quicker energy burst than complex carbohydrates. Now, however, all this has changed.

the glycemic index

The glycemic index is a scientific rating of foods based on their immediate effect on the level of glucose, or sugar, in the blood. A wide range of carbohydrate-based foods have been tested using portions that each contained 50 g (2 ounces) of carbohydrates. Each has been given a rating between 1 and 100 depending on the speed at which it releases its sugar into the blood. Carbohydrate foods that break down quickly during digestion have the highest rating on the glycemic index (70 or above). Their blood-sugar response is fast and high. Carbohydrates that break down slowly, releasing glucose gradually into the bloodstream, have a low rating (less than 55). As shown on the table on pages 12–13, many foods previously thought to release their sugars quickly into the bloodstream in fact release them quite slowly, and vice versa.

FOOD CRAVINGS AND OVEREATING

Low-GI foods release their glucose at a slow and steady rate, providing a constant supply of energy and helping to stabilize the blood-sugar level. High-GI foods have the opposite effect and cause a rapid rise in the level of sugar in the blood; the body responds by making large quantities of insulin, the sugar-lowering hormone, and releasing it into our blood, which can cause a number of problems.

Instead of simply reducing glucose in the blood to a desirable level, insulin has a tendency to send it plummeting lower than it was originally, setting up a "yo-yo" effect of sugar highs followed by extreme lows. When our blood-sugar level drops, we automatically crave fatty, sugary foods in an attempt to make it rise once more, setting up a vicious cycle of snacking and overeating.

WEIGHT GAIN

High-GI foods have a tendency to break down quickly, making them less satiating than lower-GI alternatives, and thereby increasing the likelihood of overeating. However, it is thought that the main reason why high-GI foods cause weight gain is because insulin, the sugar-lowering hormone, also promotes fat storage. In other words, the more insulin you have circulating in your blood, the more likely you are to store any excess calories that you eat as fat, and the less likely you are to burn them off as energy.

LACK OF CONCENTRATION AND MOOD SWINGS

The brain is fuelled entirely by glucose, so when the level of glucose drops as a result of high insulin production, we find it increasingly difficult to concentrate. Research shows that a low blood-sugar level is also linked to mood swings, reduced reaction times, and even depression.

DIABETES AND HEART DISEASE

Diabetes, one of the world's commonest health problems, is most prevalent in Western cultures where diets are rich in refined, highly processed foods. It is thought to be caused by the constant pressure put on the body by high-GI foods to keep blood glucose at a normal level, which may have one of two effects: either the insulin produced does not work properly or the pancreas, the organ where insulin is made, becomes less efficient at producing the hormone, sometimes giving up altogether.

Obesity and diabetes—both possible consequences of a high-GI diet—are two of the major risk factors for heart disease. In addition, a high level of insulin caused by eating high-GI meals is strongly related to increased levels of cholesterol (and of other blood fats) and high blood pressure, two more major contributory factors in heart disease.

HOW RELIABLE IS THE GLYCEMIC INDEX?

Although it is a very useful tool, the glycemic index has two significant drawbacks. The first is that fatty foods often have a low-GI rating. This is because fat has the effect of slowing down the rate of digestion. However, this does not mean that fatty foods should be eaten freely since—no matter how low-GI your diet may be—if you consume large amounts of fat you will gain weight and risk health problems.

Second, the glycemic index does not take into account the quantities of foods people are likely to eat at any given time. In other words, the GI of an apple or a portion of pasta remains the same whether you eat one or 20! This is because of the way the tests were carried out when the index was developed.

To enable valid comparisons to be made between foods, volunteers were given portions of foods that each contained 50 g (2 ounces) of usable carbohydrate. For example, pasta is a high-carbohydrate food, therefore the volunteers would not have had to eat very much of it in order to obtain the necessary 50 g. However, pumpkin is very low in carbohydrates, so the subjects would have needed to eat about 2.5 kq (5 pounds) of pumpkins to obtain the necessary 50 g—not something that most people are likely to do in daily life! Therefore, although pumpkin appears to be a high GI-food, when it is eaten in "normal" quantities, the carbohydrate content is so small that it is unlikely to have any significant effect on the level of glucose in the blood. Conversely, if eaten in large quantities, some low-GI foods, such as pasta or lentils, will send the blood glucose level soaring. It is because of this that the glycemic load measurement was devised.

the glycemic load

The glycemic load (GL) is a more sophisticated measure than the glycemic index in that it takes account of the amount of carbohydrate in a normal-sized portion. It is calculated by multiplying the amount of carbohydrate contained in a normal-sized portion by the GI of the food and dividing the result by 100. (Don't worry—all the recipes and meal ideas in this book have already been formulated to be low GI/GL, so there is no need to do the calculation yourself.) For example, pumpkin has a GI rating of 75, which is high, but a 80-g (3-ounce) serving of pumpkin contains just 5 g (a trace) of carbohydrate, so the GL is 5 x 75 = 375 divided by 100 = 3.75, rounded up to 4, which is considered to be low. So, when realistic portion sizes are part of the equation, pumpkin goes from being a high-GI food to a low-GL food, and therefore gets the green light as part of a healthy, balanced diet. Note that GL values are much lower numerically than those of GI. A GL value of 10 or less is low; a value of 11–19 is medium; a value of 20 or more is high.

GI OR GL?

The strength of the GL measurement lies in its ability to identify those foods that are the exceptions to the GI rule—such as foods that appear to be fast-releasing but when eaten in normal quantities are in fact slow-releasing. It also helps to remind us that everything should be eaten in moderation. However, as with the GI, it should not be used in isolation to assess nutritional value since this could result in a diet that is high in fat and protein and low in carbohydrates. Most dieticians and nutritionists agree that the healthiest approach is to favor a combination of low-GI and low-GL foods while keeping portion sizes in check and fat consumption low.

THE "YO-YO" EFFECT

Do you crave something sweet in the middle of the morning or afternoon, or soon after a large meal? This is probably a result of the "yo-yo" effect on your blood-sugar level. Eating a lunch of high-GI foods, such as sandwiches or a baked potato, sends blood-sugar levels soaring. Insulin kicks in, causing them to drop suddenly, and by mid-afternoon you are not only feeling tired, lethargic and lacking in concentration but you are craving something sweet to give you a much needed boost. This may also happen shortly after an evening meal, when you find yourself heading back to the kitchen for a dessert, some chocolate cookies, or a glass of wine.

popular foods with their GI and GL ratings

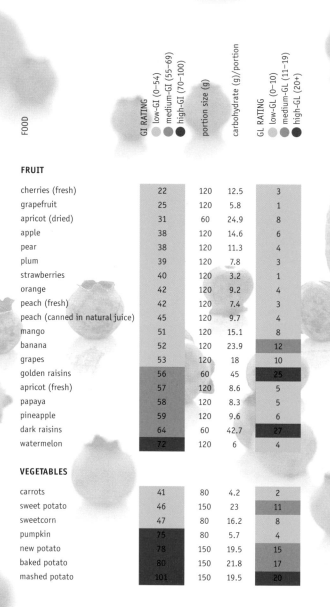

FOOD	GI RATING (low-GI 0–54 / medium-GI 55–69 / high-GI 70–100)	portion size (g)	carbohydrate (g)/portion	GL RATING (low-GL 0–10 / medium-GL 11–19 / high-GL 20+)
FRUIT				
cherries (fresh)	22	120	12.5	3
grapefruit	25	120	5.8	1
apricot (dried)	31	60	24.9	8
apple	38	120	14.6	6
pear	38	120	11.3	4
plum	39	120	7.8	3
strawberries	40	120	3.2	1
orange	42	120	9.2	4
peach (fresh)	42	120	7.4	3
peach (canned in natural juice)	45	120	9.7	4
mango	51	120	15.1	8
banana	52	120	23.9	12
grapes	53	120	18	10
golden raisins	56	60	45	25
apricot (fresh)	57	120	8.6	5
papaya	58	120	8.3	5
pineapple	59	120	9.6	6
dark raisins	64	60	42.7	27
watermelon	72	120	6	4
VEGETABLES				
carrots	41	80	4.2	2
sweet potato	46	150	23	11
sweetcorn	47	80	16.2	8
pumpkin	75	80	5.7	4
new potato	78	150	19.5	15
baked potato	80	150	21.8	17
mashed potato	101	150	19.5	20

FOOD	GI RATING (low-GI 0–54 / medium-GI 55–69 / high-GI 70–100)	portion size (g)	carbohydrate (g)/portion	GL RATING (low-GL 0–10 / medium-GL 11–19 / high-GL 20+)
BREAKFAST CEREALS				
oatmeal (rolled oats and water)	42	250	20.3	9
granola (toasted)	43	30	17	7
porridge (instant)	65	250	20.3	13
BREADS/CRACKERS				
tortilla (wheat)	30	50	20.7	6
pumpernickel	50	30	13.4	7
tortilla (corn)	52	50	20.7	11
pita bread (whole-wheat)	56	60	27.8	16
whole-grain rye bread	58	30	13.3	8
croissant	67	57	22	15
light rye bread	68	30	13.5	10
pita bread (white, mini)	68	30	15.4	10
crumpet	69	50	19.5	13
pita bread (white)	69	60	30.7	21
white bread	70	30	13.4	10
Melba toast	70	30	21.8	15
whole-wheat bread	71	30	11.4	8
bagel	72	70	35.5	26
rice cakes	74	25	18.5	15
baguette (white, plain)	95	85	43	4

> ### FRUIT AND VEGETABLES
>
> *Aim to eat at least three or four different servings of vegetables a day and two to three servings of fruit, and try to eat as many different-colored ones as possible to make sure you are getting plenty of disease-fighting antioxidants.*

GRAINS/PASTAS

FOOD	GI RATING	portion size (g)	carbohydrate (g)/portion	GL RATING
barley	25	150	31.7	8
vermicelli	35	180	45.4	16
ravioli (meat)	39	180	38.3	15
fettuccine	40	180	46.1	18
noodles (rice, fresh)	40	180	38.5	15
spaghetti (wholemeal, boiled)	42	180	44.3	19
spaghetti (white. boiled)	44	180	44.3	19
macaroni	45	180	44.3	20
linguine (thick)	46	180	44.3	20
bulgur	48	150	25.8	12
linguine (thin)	52	180	44.3	23
buckwheat	54	150	28.8	16
long grain rice (white)	54	150	42	23
wild rice	57	150	29.1	17
basmati rice (white)	58	150	42	24
noodles (rice, dried, boiled)	61	180	38.5	23
couscous	65	150	35	23
brown rice	67	150	47.7	21
arborio rice	69	150	42	29
glutinous white rice	98	150	42	41
jasmine rice	109	150	42	46

PULSES

FOOD	GI RATING	portion size (g)	carbohydrate (g)/portion	GL RATING
soy beans (canned)	14	150	4.40	.6
lentils (red, green, and brown)	27	150	14.9	4
butter beans (canned)	36	150	11.48	4
white beans	38	150	19.8	8
baked beans	40	150	16.8	7
chickpeas (canned)	40	150	20.6	8
kidney beans	43	150	14.9	6
lima beans	79	80	5.2	4

DAIRY FOODS

FOOD	GI RATING	portion size (g)	carbohydrate (g)/portion	GL RATING
yogurt (fruit with artificial sweetener)	14	200	11.6	2
milk (whole)	27	258	12.1	4
milk (skim)	32	258	13	4
yogurt (low-fat, fruit)	33	200	33	11
ice cream (low-fat)	41	50	9.5	4
pudding	43	100	20	9
ice cream (full-fat)	61	50	9	5

SNACK FOODS/CANDIES

FOOD	GI RATING	portion size (g)	carbohydrate (g)/portion	GL RATING
peanuts	14	50	4.6	0.6
mixed nuts and raisins	21	50	15.5	3
cashew nuts	25	50	12.3	3
mixed nuts (roasted)	27	50	10.3	3
chocolate (milk)	42	50	31	13
corn chips	42	50	26.1	11
sponge cake	46	63	36.6	7
chocolate (semisweet)	49	50	31	15
honey	55	10	8.2	5
potato chips (plain, salted)	57	50	23.8	14
granola bar (commercial)	58	30	19.3	11
pizza (cheese)	60	100	34.6	21
table sugar	68	10	10	7
popcorn	72	20	6.4	5
french fries	75	150	66.8	50
doughnut	76	47	18.8	14
jelly beans	78	30	24.4	19
pretzels	83	30	19.4	16

DRINKS

FOOD	GI RATING	portion size (g)	carbohydrate (g)/portion	GL RATING
apple juice (unsweetened)	40	262	26.5	11
pineapple juice (unsweetened)	46	262	27.1	13
grapefruit juice (unsweetened)	48	262	15.7	8
orange juice (unsweetened)	53	262	18.7	10
cola	58	262	27.1	16

GI RATING: low-GI (0–54), medium-GI (55–69), high-GI (70–100)
GL RATING: low-GL (0–10), medium-GL (11–19), high-GL (20+)

the benefits of a low GI/GL diet

If you switch to a lower GI/GL diet, you will almost immediately feel more energetic as your blood-glucose level stabilizes and you are freed from the effect of extreme highs followed by debilitating lows. Your brain relies totally on blood glucose for fuel so you will notice an improvement in your concentration as you eradicate the sugar lows associated with a high-GI diet. Your mood and feeling of general well-being are likely to improve too, since these are also closely linked with the blood-sugar level, which is why some people feel irritable when hungry.

People who switch to a low-GI/GL diet tend automatically to reduce the number of calories they consume. This is because calorie-dense, fatty, sugary foods are replaced with low-calorie fruits, vegetables, beans, and whole grains—all of which are far more filling, too. So food cravings and hunger pangs will reduce, and the fact that you are producing less insulin and eating fewer calories will instigate weight loss if you have weight to lose.

In the medium term, your intake of vitamins, minerals, and other essential nutrients will increase as you eat more nutrient-dense foods in the form of fruit, vegetables, oily fish, nuts, seeds, and beans. There is also overwhelming evidence that eating plenty of fruit and vegetables can help to reduce the risk of many serious diseases. Indeed, by switching to a lower GI/GL diet you can reduce your likelihood of developing diabetes, heart disease, cancer, and other life-threatening conditions by as much as 50%.

FIVE WAYS TO CHANGE TO A LOW GI/GL DIET

When preparing a meal, aim for the following nutritional balance:

• One-third high-quality protein such as fish, chicken, turkey, and lean red meats, or beans if you are vegetarian.

• One-third fruit and vegetables—eat at least seven servings of fruit and vegetables every day.

• One-third low-GI/GL carbohydrates such as beans, oats, pasta, brown basmati rice, couscous, bulgur wheat, rye bread or whole-grain breads.

Make as much of your own food as possible

Use a selection of good cookbooks to help you to adjust to this new way of eating and to inspire you to make more of your meals yourself instead of relying on store-bought products that are likely to be much higher in fat, salt, sugar, and other additives.

Don't overeat

Keep portion sizes and meals small and avoid long gaps between eating. Aim to eat five times a day—three small main meals with a snack in the middle of the morning and another one in the middle of the afternoon.

Powerfood snack ideas

• low-fat yogurt

• a handful of seeds or nuts

• fresh fruit, particularly low-GI fruits such as apples, pears, cherries, plums, and oranges

• a small whole-wheat pita bread, peanut butter, and banana

• vegetable batons dipped in hummus

• rye bread with a thin scraping of blue cheese topped with fresh grapes

• a slice of fruit loaf

• a roast chicken drumstick

THE BREAKFAST IMPERATIVE

If you are embarking on a low-GI/GL eating plan, breakfast is probably the most important meal of the day since it "breaks the fast" of your previous night's sleep, helping to restore the level of glucose, or sugar, in your blood and refuel your body ready for the day ahead—so never be tempted to skip it.

Nutritional studies have shown that people who skip breakfast miss out on many vital nutrients such as calcium, iron, and other minerals, vitamins, fiber, whole grains, protein, and carbohydrates which they are unlikely to make up for during the rest of the day.

WHOLE GRAINS, NUTS, AND SEEDS

Because nuts are high in fat, it is often assumed by people trying to lose weight that they should be avoided. This is not true. Nuts have a very low GI rating, which makes them filling, and many are great sources of essential fatty acids—the only fats that cannot be made in the body and have to come from outside sources. An adequate intake of essential fatty acids may help to prevent or control ailments such as heart disease, cancer, immune system deficiencies, arthritis, skin complaints, and menopausal symptoms. Whole grains (grains that contain the entire grain kernel—the bran, germ, and endosperm) have been shown to reduce the risks of heart disease, stroke, cancer, diabetes, and obesity.

Keep your fat intake low

Minimize your intake of commercially prepared foods and meals, cakes, cookies, potato chips, chocolate, fatty dressings and sauces, and high-fat dairy foods. Eat two to three servings a day of low-fat dairy foods such as skim milk, low-fat cheese, sour cream, low-fat yogurt, and cottage cheese; these are great sources of bone-strengthening calcium.

Substitute sugary drinks with fresh fruit juices, skim milk, and water

Sugary drinks, especially sports drinks, can have a GI rating as high as 95 and often contain a lot of empty calories. Tea and coffee can block vitamin and mineral absorption, so limit these to two to three cups a day. Added sugar, which has a GI rating of 65, will also significantly raise blood sugar level. Fresh, unsweetened fruit juices, skim milk, and water are far better alternatives, scoring much lower on the glycemic index. Fruit juices also contain extra vitamins and minerals and skim milk is a good source of calcium.

BEANS

Plan meals around beans, peas, and lentils instead of potatoes or high-GI rice options such as the easy-cook varieties. Beans are slow-releasing and nutrient-dense, providing protein, fiber, iron, calcium, folate, and soluble fiber (the type that really helps to lower cholesterol levels). They are also an excellent source of phytoestrogens, which can help to reduce the risk of many lifestyle diseases, including certain cancers, and help to control menopausal symptoms and increase the ability of the immune system to fight infections.

SEVEN WAYS TO LOWER THE GI/GL RATING OF YOUR SNACKS AND MEALS

Keep portions small

If you are eating a high-rated GI/GL food, keep the portion small and, wherever possible, combine a high-rated food with a low-rated food since this will lower the overall GI/GL rating of the meal.

Eat protein with carbohydrates

High-protein foods, such as lean meat, chicken, or fish, tend to slow the rate at which a meal is digested and thereby lower the overall GI/GL rating of the meal.

Choose vegetables first

Too many meals are based on carbohydrate-rich foods such as rice, pasta, baked potatoes, or fries. Instead, start by planning your meal around the vegetables you hope to use, then introduce protein-rich foods such as meat, fish, or beans, and then the carbohydrate-rich foods.

Use beans whenever possible

Try puréeing beans to make sauces, cooking them in stews and casseroles, serving them with fresh herbs as side dishes, adding them to salads, making them into dips, or using mashed beans or cooked lentils in place of mashed potatoes.

Keep cooking times to a minimum

Cooked foods often have a higher GI/GL than uncooked foods so make sure your pasta is al dente and your vegetables are cooked for the shortest time possible. This will also help to retain their vitamins and minerals.

Keep foods as chunky as possible

The more processed, chopped, and cooked a meal is, the quicker it is likely to breakdown after eating.

Add acids

Acid foods such as vinegar, lemon juice, vinaigrette dressing, acidic fruit and fruit juices slow down the rate at which the stomach empties and thereby lower the GI/GL rating of a meal. Note that commercially prepared vinaigrettes often contain too much fat, so make your own instead (see page 54 for some quick and easy recipe ideas).

HIGH-RATED GI/GL FOODS AND WHOLE-GRAIN ALTERNATIVES

white rice—**brown rice, wild rice**

white pasta salad—**buckwheat, bulgur wheat**

white breads—**rye breads, whole-wheat breads**

ready-to-eat breakfast cereals such as corn flakes—**porridge made from rolled oats, cereals made from 100 percent whole-wheat, or muesli**

white flour tortillas—**whole-wheat tortillas**

Other whole grains include **millet, quinoa, sorghum, triticale, whole-grain barley, whole-grain cornmeal**

PROTEIN

Eat plenty of good-quality protein, such as fish, lean red meats, chicken, and turkey, and aim to eat oily fish three times a week.

Good-quality proteins not only provide all the building blocks needed to make strong healthy bodies but they have the added advantage of helping to lower the GI/GL rating of a snack or meal.

Oily fish, such as mackerel, sardines, herring, trout, fresh (not canned) tuna and salmon, are excellent sources of essential fatty acids, the only fats that cannot be made in the body. Research has shown that just one regular weekly serving of oily fish can reduce the tendency of the blood to clot and thereby lower an individual's likelihood of suffering a fatal heart attack by as much as 40% as compared with a person who never eats oily fish.

Sample 7-day power-eating, weight-loss plan

Use this chart to devise an easy, delicious, and power-packed eating plan that'll help you lose weight, too. The daily calories number about 1500, the maximum needed by a woman who wants to lose weight. To increase calorie intake (for a woman not wishing to lose weight or for a man, for example), just increase portion sizes slightly or add one or two healthy snacks.

An average woman needs about 2000 calories a day; an average man about 2500. To lose weight, we must reduce this intake slightly, by about 500 calories per day (to 1500 for a woman and 2000 for a man). Lowering intake much more than that can result in loss of lean muscle tissue rather than fat; it can also lead to hunger pangs and fatigue.

Don't forget to keep up your fluid intake, too, by drinking at least 8 glasses of water a day.

	DAY 1	DAY 2	DAY 3
BREAKFAST	cinnamon porridge (calories: 447) *page 25* glass of freshly squeezed fruit juice (Calories: 111 approx.) total calories : 558	maple nut crunch cereal (calories: 288) *page 27* glass of freshly squeezed fruit juice (calories: 111 approx.) total calories: 399	spiced pear, apricot, and fig compote (calories: 346) *page 25* glass of freshly squeezed fruit juice (calories: 111 approx.) total calories: 457
SNACK	large handful of blueberries and a low-fat fruit yogurt (calories: 155)	1 apple and a small bunch of grapes (calories: 107)	cranberry and almond breakfast bar (calories: 162) *page 26*
LUNCH	italian bean and vegetable soup (calories: 114) *page 35*	tuna crunch open sandwich (calories: 278) *page 40*	ribbon vegetable and hummus wraps (calories: 235) *page 45*
SNACK	1 fruit and nut bar (calories: 126) *page 118*	cheese and scallion whole-wheat scone topped with low-fat spread and sliced fresh tomato (calories: 183) *page 125*	1 apple (calories: 47)
SUPPER	tarragon chicken casserole (calories: 292) *page 59*	roasted vegetable and rice gratin (calories: 286) *page 60*	spiced salmon with chickpea dhal (calories: 517) *page 67*
DESSERT	citrus fruit salad with rose water and pistachios (calories: 249) *page 107*	white chocolate and raspberry fool (calories: 170) *page 112*	cranberry and raspberry jelly (calories: 119) *page 109*
CALORIES	calories: 1494	calories: 1423	calories: 1537

DAY 4	DAY 5	DAY 6	DAY 7
mango, raspberry, and orange smoothie (calories: 223) *page 33* two slices whole-grain toast with low-fat spread (calories: 150) total calories: 373	florentine baked eggs with 2 slices of whole-grain toast (calories: 234) *page 29* glass of freshly squeezed orange juice (calories: 111 approx.) total calories: 345	huevos rancheros with 2 slices of whole-grain toast (calories: 292) *page 29* glass of freshly squeezed fruit juice (calories: 111 approx.) total calories: 423	oat hotcakes with warm blueberries (calories: 177) *page 31* banana (calories: 108) glass of freshly squeezed fruit juice (calories: 111 approx.) total calories: 396
blueberry and apple muffin (calories: 144) *page 30*	1 glass of skim milk and a banana (calories: 176)	1 slice spiced apple loaf cake (calories: 173) *page 123*	1 large orange (calories: 77)
smoked haddock and puy lentil chowder (calories: 244) *page 37*	prawn and avocado open sandwich (Calories: 244) *page 40*	grilled chicken and roasted pepper salad (calories: 315) *page 49*	tacos with beans (calories: 230) *page 57* low-fat fruit yogurt (calories: 117)
1 low-fat yogurt with 1 chopped banana and 25 g mixed nuts (calories: 377)	passionfruit and papaya blitz (calories: 223) *page 32*	1 large bowl of fresh strawberries and 2 chopped kiwi fruits (calories: 112)	2 cherry and hazelnut oat cookies (calories: 138) *page 119*
tuna steaks with mango and chile salsa (calories: 231) *page 103*	goulash meatballs (calories: 260) *page 71*	hot and sour prawn noodle bowl (calories: 312) *page 63*	greek lemon chicken kebabs (calories: 220) *page 65*
chocolate dipped fruits (calories: 106) *page 110*	spiced berry compote (calories: 178) *page 110*	passionfruit yogurt ice (calories: 127) *page 108*	pan-fried caribbean bananas (calories: 264) *page 116*
calories: 1475	calories: 1426	calories: 1462	calories: 1442

your questions answered

Wouldn't it be simpler to eliminate carbohydrate-based foods from my diet altogether?

No. Carbohydrates are very important in the diet because they are broken down to form glucose and glycogen.

• Fat can be burned and used as energy only if glucose is present. If we don't eat enough carbohydrate, our body responds by breaking down lean muscle tissue and turning it into glucose. This is to be avoided, since a loss of lean muscle tissue automatically causes a decline in metabolic rate, which in turn causes us to gain weight.

• The brain depends on glucose for healthy functioning.

• If we fail to eat enough carbohydrate, our glycogen stores become depleted, leaving us feeling tired, shaky, and often experiencing headaches.

• Carbohydrate foods are natural appetite suppressants.

• Carbohydrate is less likely than dietary fat to be stored as fat on the body.

Why don't foods such as meat, fish, chicken, and avocados appear in the GI/GL food listings?

The glycemic index is a measure of how quickly the carbohydrate content of a food is broken down and released into the blood. Foods such as meat, fish, chicken, avocado, and nuts contain no, or very little, carbohydrate. This is also true of many fruits and vegetables.

Can I eat as much low-GI food as I like?

No. Just because a food has a low-GI rating it doesn't mean that it can be eaten in large quantities, as this can still lead to weight gain, especially if the food is high in fat and calories. There are three main factors to consider when choosing which foods should make up the majority of your meals:

• The GI rating of the food.

• The fat content of the food.

• The amount of the food that you are eating—even low-GI foods can stimulate big releases of insulin if eaten in large quantities

I notice that some fruits and carbohydrates have a high GI value—does this mean I should avoid them?

Not necessarily. Check their GL values, too. Some foods that have a high GI rating may have a low GL rating (see pages 12–13).

What effect does a low-GI/GL diet have on children?

Children can suffer from the yo-yo effect in the same way as adults (see page 11). A sudden surge in a child's blood glucose level will often manifest itself in excessive nervous energy, running around, shouting, crying, tantrums, and general disruptive behavior. A low-GI/GL diet can help make sure that the blood glucose level remains constant, enhancing a child's ability to concentrate, learn, interact, play constructively, and sleep. Reducing the GI/GL rating of a child's diet simply involves cutting back on overprocessed, fatty, sugary foods and drinks and replacing them with fresh fruit and vegetables, beans, lower-GI/GL alternatives to the usual high-GI/GL breads, rices, and cereals, and adding plenty of good-quality lean meats and fish.

Can I still eat in restaurants while I am following a low GI/GL eating plan?

Although it can be more difficult to maintain a low GI/GL diet when eating out, it certainly isn't impossible and it need not be complicated either. Don't be intimidated by a new menu. Remember that you have three main aims:

• To keep the GI/GL rating of your meal as low as possible.

• To keep the fat content (particularly the saturated fat content) of your meal as low as possible.

• To avoid overeating. Ask for smaller portions and choose either a starter or a dessert to go with your main course rather than both.

Avoid or eat very little of:

• Foods that are particularly fatty—such as fried foods, creamy sauces, and cream-laden desserts.

• Foods with a high GI/GL rating—such as most forms of potato, including mashed, fried, and baked, most forms of rice (other than basmati), most breads, and other highly refined carbohydrate-based foods including sugary drinks and desserts.

Choose instead:

• Pasta- and noodle-based dishes.

• Vegetables—either go for a vegetable-based main course or order some extra vegetable side dishes to replace the fries, rice, or potatoes that you might ordinarily have had.

• Salad—either as an entrée, an appetizer, or a side dish.

• Protein-based foods—such as lean meat, fish, chicken, and beans. The protein they provide will help to lower the GI/GL rating of your meal as a whole

• Fruit-based desserts—instead of desserts laden with refined flour and sugar (and fat).

Is there anything else I can do, apart from switching to a low-GI/GL eating plan, to improve health, increase vitality, and enhance weight loss?

Yes—get moving! Research shows that activity and exercise not only burns calories, helping you lose weight more effectively, but it also increases the efficiency of insulin in the body, thereby lowering the risk of many of the health problems associated with a high GI/GL diet.

Aim to do a minimum of 30 minutes aerobic exercise three times a week such as walking, swimming, running, cycling, or even dancing. In addition to this, maximize every opportunity you have to be more active. Park on the opposite side of the parking lot from the supermarket entrance, walk the children to school, cycle to and from work, go for a quick jog around the park first thing in the morning, at lunchtime, or in the evening, wash your car and the windows of your home by hand, do some gardening—anything that gets you moving.

Should I avoid all high-GI/Gl foods?

No. There are several reasons for this.

• For non-diabetics, there are times when a rapid increase in blood sugar level (and the corresponding increase in insulin) may be desirable. For example, after strenuous physical activity, insulin helps to move glucose into muscle cells, where it aids tissue repair. Because of this, some coaches and physical trainers recommend the consumption of high-GI/GL foods, such as sports drinks, immediately after exercise to speed recovery.

• Research shows that a just two low-GI/GL meals a day may be enough to stabilize the blood glucose level and thereby reduce the risk of weight gain and many of the major lifestyle diseases.

• The speed at which a high-GI/GL food releases its sugar into your bloodstream can be reduced by eating it with other foods, particularly those high in fat and protein, although of course, no matter how low the GI/GL rating of the carbohydrates you consume, if they are all high in fat they will do little for your health or your waistline!

the recipes

The nutritional analysis given for each recipe refers to one serving.

Unless otherwise stated, all eggs used in the recipes are large and all spoon measurements are level.

breakfasts

spiced pear, apricot, and fig compote

2/3 **cup unsweetened apple juice**

1 **cup ready-to-eat dried apricots, halved**

1/2 **cup ready-to-eat dried figs, halved**

8 **cardamom pods, lightly crushed**

2 **pears, cored and sliced into wedges**

TO SERVE

3 1/2 **oz. low-fat Greek (strained) yogurt**

2 **teaspoons pumpkin seeds**

SERVES 2

Put all the ingredients in a saucepan, bring to a simmer and cook, covered, for 2–4 minutes, depending on the ripeness of the pears. Transfer to a bowl and let cool. Cover and chill overnight in the refrigerator.

To serve, discard the cardamom pods and divide the compote between serving bowls. Top each bowlful with half of the Greek yogurt and the pumpkin seeds.

cinnamon porridge

1/3 **cup old-fashioned rolled oats**

1 **tablespoon wheat germ**

1/2 **teaspoon ground cinnamon**

2/3 **cup skim milk**

a pinch of salt

2 **tablespoons whole almonds, chopped**

1/2 **cup fresh raspberries**

1/2 **medium banana, sliced**

2 **teaspoons maple syrup or honey, to serve**

SERVES 1

Put the oats, wheat germ, and cinnamon in a saucepan, then add the milk, salt, and 1/2 cup of water. Cook over medium heat for about 5 minutes or until the oats are tender and the porridge has thickened.

Pour the porridge into a bowl and top with the almonds, raspberries, and banana, then drizzle the maple syrup or honey over the top to serve.

cranberry and almond breakfast bars

These energy-boosting breakfast bars are great for the school run in the morning, and will give an instant pick-me-up on the way home in the afternoon, too. Vary the fruits and nuts—try combinations such as apricot and pistachio, cherry and pecan, or blueberry and hazelnut.

1/2 **cup whole almonds**

1/3 **cup polyunsaturated margarine**

3 **tablespoons honey**

1/3 **cup packed brown sugar**

1 2/3 **cups old-fashioned rolled oats**

1/2 **cup whole-wheat flour, preferably stone-ground**

1/2 **teaspoon baking powder**

a pinch of salt

1/3 **cup dried cranberries**

1 **banana**

3 1/2 **oz. low-fat plain yogurt**

1 **egg, beaten**

1 **eating apple, cored, and coarsely grated**

a baking pan, 8 x 9 1/2 inches, lined with baking parchment

MAKES 14

Spread the almonds out evenly on a baking sheet and toast in a preheated oven at 350°F for 4–5 minutes until golden, then chop.

Meanwhile, heat the margarine, honey, and sugar in a saucepan until melted. Let cool slightly.

In a large bowl, stir the almonds together with the oats, flour, baking powder, salt, and cranberries. Mash the banana and mix with the yogurt, egg, and grated apple. Mix this and the melted margarine mixture into the oats. Smooth into the prepared pan and bake for 20 minutes or until golden brown and firm.

Remove the baked mixture from the oven, lift out of the tin, and let cool on a wire rack. Peel off the baking parchment and cut the oat mixture into bars. The breakfast bars can be stored in an airtight container for up to 3 days or can be frozen.

NUTRITIONAL INFORMATION
Calories: **162**
Fat: **5.5 g (0.7 g saturated)**
Protein: **5 g**
Carbohydrate: **27 g**

NUTRITIONAL INFORMATION
Calories: 288
Fat: 10 g (1.2 g saturated)
Protein: 9 g
Carbohydrate: 41 g

maple nut crunch cereal

This homemade version of crunch cluster-type cereal has a lovely toasty flavor. Serve simply with chilled milk or add to low-fat yogurt with some fresh fruit.

1²/₃ cups old-fashioned rolled oats

3 tablespoons pumpkin seeds

1¹/₂ tablespoons sunflower seeds

2 tablespoons whole almonds, chopped

2 tablespoons whole hazelnuts, chopped

3 tablespoons pure maple syrup

¹/₂ cup ready-to-eat dried apricots, chopped

¹/₃ cup golden raisins

a large baking sheet, lined with baking parchment

SERVES 6

Mix the oats, seeds, and nuts together in a large bowl, add the maple syrup and stir well until evenly coated. Spread out on the lined baking sheet and bake in a preheated oven at 400°F for 10–12 minutes, until toasted and golden brown.

Let cool, then mix with the dried fruits and store in an airtight container for up to 4 weeks.

florentine baked eggs

Drinking a large glass of freshly squeezed orange juice with this dish will maximize absorption of iron from the spinach.

NUTRITIONAL INFORMATION
Calories: **234**
Fat: **7 g (3 g saturated)**
Protein: **14 g**
Carbohydrate: **26 g**

8 oz. baby spinach, rinsed

freshly grated nutmeg

4 very fresh eggs

4 tablespoons low-fat sour cream

2 tablespoons Parmesan cheese, freshly grated

sea salt and freshly ground black pepper

8 slices of whole-grain toast, to serve

4 ramekins, lightly greased

a small roasting pan

SERVES 4

Put the kettle on to boil. Cook the spinach in a covered pan until wilted, stirring once or twice. Drain off any excess liquid and season with nutmeg, salt, and pepper to taste.

Divide the spinach between the prepared ramekins. Make a hollow in the spinach and break an egg into each one. Season lightly, then top each egg with a spoonful of sour cream and a sprinkling of Parmesan cheese.

Put the ramekins in the roasting pan and pour boiling water around them to come halfway up the sides. Bake in a preheated oven at 350°F for 14–16 minutes, depending on how soft you like the yolks. Bear in mind that the eggs will carry on cooking after they have come out of the oven. Serve immediately with 2 slices of whole-grain toast per serving.

huevos rancheros

Softly poached eggs with spicy tomato sauce make this a great brunch dish.

1 tablespoon soy sauce

1 onion, chopped

1 green bell pepper, deseeded and chopped

1 small fresh red chile, deseeded and finely chopped

1 garlic clove, crushed

1 teaspoon ground cumin

14 oz. canned chopped tomatoes

2 very fresh eggs

2 tablespoons chopped fresh cilantro, to serve

4 slices of whole-grain toast, to serve

SERVES 2

Heat the soy sauce and 2 tablespoons of water in a nonstick frying pan. Add the onion and cook for 5 minutes until the liquid has evaporated and the onion has softened. Stir in the pepper, chile, garlic, and ground cumin and cook for 1 minute.

Tip in the tomatoes, season, and simmer, uncovered, for 5 minutes until the sauce has thickened. Make 2 hollows in the sauce and break an egg into each. Reduce the heat, cover, and cook for 5 minutes until the eggs are soft set. Scatter with cilantro and serve with 2 slices of toast per serving.

NUTRITIONAL INFORMATION
Calories: **292**
Fat: **8 g (2.5 g saturated)**
Protein: **16 g**
Carbohydrate: **39 g**

blueberry and apple muffins

To help increase your intake of vitamins, minerals, fiber, and energy-giving calories, eat these muffins, or the hotcakes opposite, accompanied by one or two pieces of fresh fruit.

1¹/₃ cups whole-wheat flour, preferably stone-ground

1¹/₂ teaspoons baking powder

¹/₂ teaspoon salt

¹/₂ teaspoon ground cinnamon

¹/₂ cup old-fashioned rolled oats

1 cup fresh blueberries

1 eating apple, cored and diced

1 cup low-fat plain yogurt

1 egg, beaten

6 tablespoons honey

3 tablespoons safflower oil

¹/₂ teaspoon baking soda

a 12-hole nonstick muffin pan, lightly greased

MAKES 12

Sift the flour, baking powder, salt, and cinnamon into a mixing bowl, tipping in any bran left in the sieve. Reserve 2 tablespoons of the oats for the top of the muffins, then stir the remainder into the flour, followed by the blueberries and apple.

In a separate bowl, beat the yogurt, egg, honey, and safflower oil together. Mix in the baking soda, then immediately add the wet ingredients to the dry ingredients bowl. Stir together briefly, but don't overmix or the muffins will be tough.

Spoon the batter into the prepared muffin pan and scatter the reserved oats on top. Bake in a preheated oven at 375°F for 20 minutes, until the muffins are risen and golden. Serve warm, or let cool on a wire rack and store in an airtight container for up to 3 days. The muffins can also be frozen.

> **NUTRITIONAL INFORMATION**
> Calories: **144**
> Fat: **4 g (0.75 g saturated)**
> Protein: **5 g**
> Carbohydrate: **23 g**

oat hotcakes with warm blueberries

Blueberries are packed with antioxidants, making them powerful disease-fighters.

HOTCAKES

1 cup whole-wheat flour, preferably stone-ground

2 teaspoons baking powder

$^1/_8$ teaspoon of salt

4 teaspoons sugar

$^1/_3$ cup old-fashioned rolled oats

2 eggs, lightly beaten

$^2/_3$ cup skim milk

BLUEBERRIES

3 cups frozen or fresh blueberries

grated zest and freshly squeezed juice of $^1/_2$ unwaxed lemon

2 tablespoons sugar

2 teaspoons cornstarch or arrowroot

6 tablespoons Greek (strained) yogurt, to serve

SERVES 6

To make the batter, sift the flour, baking powder, and salt into a bowl, tipping in any bran left in the sieve. Stir in the sugar and oats, make a well in the center, then add the eggs and milk. Mix together gradually until you have a smooth batter.

Heat a lightly greased, nonstick frying pan over medium heat and cook 4–6 hotcakes at a time, using 1 tablespoon of batter for each. Cook for 60–90 seconds on one side until the top is bubbly and almost set, then flip over and cook for 30–40 seconds to brown the other side. Keep warm in a low oven while you cook the remaining hotcakes, to make a total of 24.

Meanwhile, put the blueberries in a covered pan with the lemon zest and juice and sugar. Simmer for 5 minutes until softened and juicy. Blend the cornstarch with a little cold water, then mix into the hot blueberries and cook, stirring, until thickened.

Serve a stack of 4 hotcakes per person, with the warm blueberries spooned over and topped with a tablespoonful of yogurt. The hotcakes are suitable for freezing.

passionfruit and papaya blitz

1 orange

3 ice cubes

1 ripe papaya

2 ripe passionfruit, halved

SERVES 1

NUTRITIONAL INFORMATION
Calories: **223**
Fat: **0 g (0 g saturated)**
Protein: **4 g**
Carbohydrate: **55 g**

Squeeze the juice from the orange and pour into a blender, adding the pulp from the citrus squeezer, together with the ice cubes. Halve the papaya, discard the seeds, and scoop the flesh into the blender using a spoon. Blend until smooth, then stir in the seeds from the passionfruit. Mix briefly and serve in a glass.

strawberry shake

3 ice cubes

¹/₄ cup skim milk

¹/₄ cup low-fat plain or strawberry yogurt

1¹/₄ cups fresh ripe strawberries, chopped

¹/₂ banana, sliced

¹/₂ teaspoon pure vanilla extract

1 tablespoon honey

SERVES 1

NUTRITIONAL INFORMATION
Calories: **294**
Fat: **2 g (1 g saturated)**
Protein: **12 g**
Carbohydrate: **59 g**

Put all the ingredients in a blender and process until smooth. Pour into a glass and serve.

mango, raspberry, and orange smoothie

This is a great accompaniment to a couple of slices of whole-grain toast, a banana, or bowl of cereal.

1 large orange

¹⁄₂ mango, peeled, stoned, and chopped

³⁄₄ cup fresh or frozen raspberries

3 ice cubes (if using fresh berries)

SERVES 1

Squeeze the juice from the orange and pour into a blender, adding the pulp from the citrus squeezer. Add the chopped mango, raspberries, and ice cubes, if using, and blend until smooth. Pour into a glass and serve.

NUTRITIONAL INFORMATION
Calories: 139
Fat: 0 g (0 g saturated)
Protein: 4 g
Carbohydrate: 32 g

light lunches

italian bean and vegetable soup

This soup is delicious with a large chunk of stone-ground wholemeal bread.

In a large flameproof casserole or saucepan, soften the onion and garlic in ¼ cup of the broth for 5 minutes, with the lid on. Stir in the carrots, mushrooms, and zucchini, season and cook for 2 minutes. Stir in the tomato juice and the remaining broth and bring to a simmer, then cover and cook for 10 minutes.

Mix in the beans and cabbage, re-cover the pan and simmer for a further 10 minutes. Adjust the seasoning and stir in the basil just before serving.

NUTRITIONAL INFORMATION
Calories: 114
Fat: 1 g (0.1 g saturated)
Protein: 7 g
Carbohydrate: 20 g

1 onion, chopped

2 garlic cloves, crushed

5 cups low-sodium vegetable broth

2 carrots, diced

2 cups mushrooms, chopped

2 zucchini, diced

3 cups low-sodium tomato juice

14-oz. canned cannellini beans, drained and rinsed

1¼ cups shredded green cabbage

3 tablespoons chopped fresh basil

sea salt and freshly ground black pepper

a large flameproof casserole (optional)

SERVES 6

sweet potato, butterbean, tomato, and ginger soup

14 oz. canned chopped tomatoes

14 oz. canned butterbeans, drained and rinsed

1¼ lbs. sweet potatoes, peeled and diced

3 cups vegetable broth

1 teaspoon ground cumin

1 tablespoon grated fresh ginger

sea salt and freshly ground black pepper

4 teaspoons low-fat sour cream, to serve

SERVES 4

Put all the ingredients, except the sour cream, in a large saucepan. Bring to a boil, then cover and simmer for 18–20 minutes, or until the sweet potato is tender.

Transfer a third of the soup to a blender and blend until smooth, then mix this back into the saucepan. Adjust the seasoning to taste, then ladle the soup into bowls and top each serving with a teaspoon of the sour cream.

NUTRITIONAL INFORMATION
Calories: 276
Fat: 1.5 g (0.6.5 g saturated)
Protein: 12 g
Carbohydrate: 58 g

smoked haddock and green lentil chowder

This chunky soup is full of interesting flavors. Lentils not only give the soup color and texture, but they pack a powerful protein punch, while also helping to maintain a healthy digestive system and reducing cholesterol.

³/₄ **cup green lentils, preferably "Puy" lentils, rinsed**

2 leeks, rinsed and chopped

2¹/₂ cups vegetable, fish, or chicken broth

8 small new potatoes, scrubbed and diced

1¹/₄ cups skim milk

12 oz. smoked haddock fillets, skinned

2 tablespoons finely snipped fresh chives

sea salt and freshly ground black pepper

SERVES 4

Put the rinsed lentils in a saucepan, add enough boiling water to cover the lentils by 1¹/₂ inches, cover the saucepan and simmer for 15–20 minutes until tender, then drain.

Meanwhile, simmer the leeks in ¹/₄ cup of the broth in a large saucepan, covered, for 3–4 minutes until softened. Stir in the potatoes, milk, and remaining broth. Season and bring to a boil, then simmer for 15 minutes or until the potatoes are tender.

Add the smoked haddock to the saucepan and simmer for 4–5 minutes until the fish flakes easily. Lift the haddock out of the pan and break into large flakes.

Stir the lentils into the chowder, ladle into bowls, and top with the flaked smoked haddock. Add a scattering of chives and serve.

NUTRITIONAL INFORMATION
Calories: **244**
Fat: **2 g (0.5 g saturated)**
Protein: **31 g**
Carbohydrate: **27 g**

chickpea, lemon, and mint soup

This pantry-based soup couldn't be easier. It's made from a minimal number of ingredients, but has an intriguingly complex flavor.

3 x 14-oz. cans chickpeas

2 garlic cloves, crushed

grated zest and freshly squeezed juice of 2 unwaxed lemons

3 tablespoons chopped fresh mint

2 tablespoons extra virgin olive oil

sea salt and freshly ground black pepper

SERVES 4

NUTRITIONAL INFORMATION
Calories: 406
Fat: 9 g (1 g saturated)
Protein: 15 g
Carbohydrate: 67 g

Drain the liquid from the chickpeas into a pitcher, and make up to 3 cups with water. Tip 2 cans of the drained chickpeas into a food processor add the garlic, lemon zest and juice, mint, olive oil, and enough of the chickpea liquid to blend to a purée. Pour into a saucepan and stir in the remaining whole chickpeas and liquid. Season to taste and heat through for about 5 minutes until gently bubbling. Ladle into bowls and serve immediately.

tuna crunch open sandwich

1/4 cup plain yogurt

1 teaspoon whole-grain mustard

3 1/2 oz. canned tuna steak in spring water, drained and flaked

1 celery stalk, sliced

1/2 eating apple, cored and chopped

2 tablespoons walnuts or pecan nuts, chopped

2 slices seeded whole-grain bread

a handful of arugula leaves

SERVES 2

Mix the yogurt and mustard together, then stir in the tuna, celery, apple, and nuts. Divide between the slices of bread and top with the arugula leaves. Cut in half to serve.

NUTRITIONAL INFORMATION
Calories: 278
Fat: 8 g (2.8 g saturated)
Protein: 30 g
Carbohydrate: 20 g

shrimp and avocado open sandwich

2 tablespoons low-fat plain yogurt

1 tablespoon chopped fresh cilantro

grated zest and freshly squeezed juice of 1/2 unwaxed lime

1 slice seeded rye bread

1/2 ripe avocado, peeled, pitted, and sliced

2 oz. cooked peeled shrimp

sea salt and freshly ground black pepper

SERVES 1

Mix the yogurt with the cilantro and half the lime zest, and spread this over the bread. Toss the avocado and shrimp with the remaining lime zest and juice, season lightly, then pile on top of the bread. Cut in half to serve.

NUTRITIONAL INFORMATION
Calories: 244
Fat: 8 g (2 g saturated)
Protein: 18 g
Carbohydrate: 18 g

roast beef, horseradish, and spinach open sandwich

1 slice seeded rye bread

1 tablespoon low-fat plain yogurt

1 teaspoon horseradish sauce

a handful of spinach leaves, rinsed

2 oz. thinly sliced rare roast beef

sea salt and freshly ground black pepper

SERVES 1

Lightly toast the rye bread. Mix the yogurt and horseradish together with a little seasoning, and spread half onto the toast. Top with the spinach leaves and beef, then drizzle with the remaining horseradish dressing. Serve immediately.

> **NUTRITIONAL INFORMATION**
> Calories: 171
> Fat: 4 g (1 g saturated)
> Protein: 18 g
> Carbohydrate: 17 g

smoked haddock rarebit toasts

These make a satisfying light lunch accompanied by salad greens with a lemony dressing.

2 slices seeded whole-grain bread

1 egg, beaten

1 teaspoon whole-grain mustard

1/2 cup finely grated reduced-fat sharp Cheddar cheese

1 scallion, chopped

3 1/2 oz. smoked haddock fillets, skinned and chopped

2 tomatoes, sliced

sea salt and freshly ground black pepper

SERVES 2

In a toaster oven, lightly toast the bread on both sides. Mix the egg and mustard together in a bowl, then stir in the cheese, scallion, and smoked haddock. Season lightly.

Divide the tomato slices between the pieces of toast, then spoon the rarebit mixture on top. Return the toast to the toaster oven and cook for 4–5 minutes, until the rarebit topping is bubbling and golden brown.

> **NUTRITIONAL INFORMATION**
> Calories: **242**
> Fat: **7 g (3 g saturated)**
> Protein: **26 g**
> Carbohydrate: **18 g**

mini asparagus and mint frittatas

Best served at room temperature rather than warm, these make a great addition to a packed lunch. Serve with a large green salad to balance the fat content.

8 oz. fresh asparagus, trimmed and chopped

2 whole eggs, plus 3 egg whites

2 tablespoons low-fat sour cream

2 tablespoons skim milk

2 tablespoons freshly grated Parmesan cheese

2 tablespoons finely chopped fresh mint

sea salt and freshly ground black pepper

a 12-hole nonstick muffin pan

MAKES 8

Add the asparagus to a pan of lightly salted boiling water, cook for 3 minutes, then drain and refresh under cold running water. Pat dry on paper, then divide the asparagus between the prepared muffin holes.

Meanwhile, beat the whole eggs and whites together with the sour cream and milk. Stir in the Parmesan, mint, and seasoning. Pour the egg mixture over the asparagus in the muffin pan. Bake in a preheated oven at 350°F for 15 minutes until firm and lightly golden. Carefully remove the frittatas from the muffin pan and let cool slightly before serving.

NUTRITIONAL INFORMATION
Calories: **51**
Fat: **3 g (1 g saturated)**
Protein: **4 g**
Carbohydrate: **1.5 g**

chapatti wraps

These simple Indian-style flat breads can be made ahead and frozen. Warm briefly in a microwave to revive them.

1½ cups whole-wheat flour, preferably stone-ground

a pinch of sea salt

MAKES 6

Stir the flour together with the salt in a mixing bowl. Gradually mix in enough cold water (7–8 tablespoons) to give a soft but not sticky dough that comes together easily. Tip the dough out onto a lightly floured surface and knead for 4–5 minutes. Shape the dough into 6 balls and rest them under the upturned bowl for 30 minutes.

Dip each ball in a little flour and roll out to an 8-inch circle. Preheat a nonstick frying pan over medium to high heat, add one chapatti and cook for about 90 seconds, flipping over a couple of times, until the flat bread is patterned with brown spots and is cooked. Repeat with the remaining chapattis.

If you wish, you can puff up the wraps over a gas flame; use tongs to hold a chapatti over the hob, until it is lightly scorched in places and puffed up.

> **NUTRITIONAL INFORMATION**
> Calories: **103**
> Fat: **0.6 g** (0 g saturated)
> Protein: **4 g**
> Carbohydrate: **21 g**

ribbon vegetable and hummus wraps

2 chapatti wraps (see opposite)

4 tablespoons reduced-fat hummus

1 carrot

$^1/_2$ red, orange, or yellow bell pepper, deseeded and thinly sliced

a handful of watercress, rinsed

SERVES 2

Gently warm the chapatti wraps to make them more flexible, either by dry-frying for a few seconds each side in a frying pan, or in the microwave for 10 seconds on high. Spread each one with 2 tablespoons of hummus. Use a vegetable peeler to shave the carrot into ribbons, then divide these between the wraps. Add the pepper and watercress, roll up the wraps, and cut in half to serve.

NUTRITIONAL INFORMATION
Calories: **235**
Fat: **6 g (0 g saturated)**
Protein: **8.5 g**
Carbohydrate: **37 g**

niçoise pasta lunchbox

40 g whole-wheat pasta rotini

4 oz. green beans, cut into thirds

1 egg

1/3 cup imported black olives

6 1/2 oz. canned tuna steak in spring water, drained and flaked

1 cup cherry tomatoes, halved

2 small heads Bibb lettuce, leaves separated

DRESSING

1 tablespoon freshly squeezed lemon juice

1 tablespoon extra virgin olive oil

1 small garlic clove, crushed

2 heaping tablespoons chopped fresh basil

sea salt and freshly ground black pepper

SERVES 2

> **NUTRITIONAL INFORMATION**
> Calories: **256**
> Fat: **10 g (4 g saturated)**
> Protein: **29 g**
> Carbohydrate: **9 g**

Cook the pasta in a saucepan of lightly salted boiling water for about 12 minutes or until tender. Add the green beans to the pan for the last 3 minutes of cooking time. Drain the pasta and beans, then refresh briefly with cold water.

Meanwhile, add the egg to a small saucepan of cold water. Bring to a boil, then simmer for 6 minutes. Drain and rinse under cold water until cool. Peel the egg and cut in half.

Beat the dressing ingredients together with the seasoning in a mixing bowl. Mix in the pasta and beans, olives, flaked tuna, and cherry tomatoes. Divide the lettuce leaves between 2 lunchboxes or bowls and top with the Niçoise pasta, and the hard-cooked egg halves.

grilled chicken and roasted pepper salad

*This is a very colorful warm salad. The spices add
a note of smokiness to the dressing.*

**1 red and 1 yellow bell
pepper**

**5 oz. sugar snap peas,
halved diagonally**

**14 oz. canned Great
Northern beans, drained
and rinsed**

**3 plum tomatoes, cut into
wedges**

**2 x skinless and boneless
chicken breasts,
4 oz. each**

¹/₂ teaspoon olive oil

DRESSING

¹/₂ teaspoon ground cumin

a pinch of smoked paprika

**1 tablespoon freshly
squeezed lemon juice**

**2 tablespoons extra virgin
olive oil**

**sea salt and freshly ground
black pepper**

a ridged stove-top grill pan

SERVES 4

Put the peppers directly on the rack of an oven
preheated at 400°F, with a piece of foil on the
shelf below to catch any cooking juices. Roast
for 20 minutes until the skins are blackened
and blistered, then transfer to a bowl, cover,
and let stand until cool enough to handle. Peel
off the skins, discard the seeds, and cut the
flesh into ribbons.

Meanwhile, blanch the sugar snap peas in
a saucepan of lightly salted boiling water for
2 minutes, then drain and refresh with cold
water. Beat the dressing ingredients together
in a large bowl, then stir in the sugar snap peas,
beans, tomatoes, and roasted peppers.

Cut the chicken breasts in half horizontally to
make 4 escalopes, season, and brush with the
olive oil. Cook on a preheated ridged stove-top
grill pan for 2–3 minutes on each side until
cooked through. Serve the chicken on a bed of
the salad vegetables.

NUTRITIONAL INFORMATION
Calories: **315**
Fat: **7 g** (1 g saturated)
Protein: **32 g**
Carbohydrate: **32 g**

smoked mackerel and bulgur wheat salad

The creamy horseradish dressing is a fabulous complement to the richness of the smoked mackerel, while raw vegetables add crunch and color.

1/2 **cup bulgur wheat**

1 tablespoon freshly squeezed lemon juice

1 tablespoon finely snipped fresh chives

1/2 **yellow bell pepper, deseeded and diced**

8 radishes, sliced

1 1/2 **cups fresh baby spinach, rinsed**

5 oz. smoked mackerel fillets, flaked

DRESSING

3 tablespoons fat-free sour cream

2 teaspoons horseradish sauce

1 teaspoon finely snipped fresh chives

freshly ground black pepper, to serve

SERVES 2

Cook the bulgur wheat in a saucepan of lightly salted boiling water for 15 minutes or until tender. Drain, then mix with the lemon juice, chives, yellow pepper, and radishes.

Divide the spinach leaves between 2 shallow salad bowls, spoon the bulgur wheat on top, then add the flaked smoked mackerel. Mix the dressing ingredients together and drizzle over the fish. Finish with a grinding of black pepper to serve.

NUTRITIONAL INFORMATION
Calories: **331**
Fat: **15 g** (3 g saturated)
Protein: **17.5 g**
Carbohydrate: **29 g**

tonno e fagioli

12 oz. thin green beans

14 oz. canned flageolet or white kidney beans, drained and rinsed

14 oz. canned cannellini beans, drained and rinsed

$1/4$ cup mixed chopped fresh herbs (such as parsley, basil, and chives)

$6^1/2$ oz. canned tuna steak in spring water, drained and flaked

DRESSING

1 tablespoon Dijon mustard

$1^1/2$ tablespoons white wine vinegar

2 tablespoons extra virgin olive oil

1 shallot, finely chopped

4 anchovy fillets, finely chopped

SERVES 4

NUTRITIONAL INFORMATION
Calories: 346
Fat: 8 g (1 g saturated)
Protein: 40 g
Carbohydrate: 30 g

Cook the green beans in a saucepan of lightly salted boiling water for 4–5 minutes until tender. Drain and refresh with cold water. Meanwhile, mix the canned beans together with the herbs in a large bowl. Beat the dressing ingredients together with 1 tablespoon of water in a separate bowl, then mix two-thirds into the canned beans.

To serve, arrange the green beans on a serving platter and drizzle over the remaining dressing. Spoon the dressed canned beans in a mound on top of the green beans, then top with the flaked tuna.

honey and lemon salad dressing

A light and piquant fat-free salad dressing.

freshly squeezed juice of 1/2 lemon

1/2 teaspoon Dijon mustard

1 tablespoon honey

sea salt and freshly ground black pepper

SERVES 2

Beat the ingredients together in a bowl until smooth, or shake together in a clean screw-top jar.

> **NUTRITIONAL INFORMATION**
> Calories: **58**
> Fat: **0 g (0 g saturated)**
> Protein: **0.7 g**
> Carbohydrate: **14 g**

balsamic vinaigrette

A thicker salad dressing with a robust flavor.

1 small garlic clove, crushed

1 teaspoon whole-grain mustard

1 tablespoon balsamic vinegar

1/2 tablespoon walnut or extra virgin olive oil

1 teaspoon honey

sea salt and freshly ground black pepper

SERVES 2

Beat the ingredients together in a bowl until smooth, or shake together in a clean screw-top jar.

> **NUTRITIONAL INFORMATION**
> Calories: **63**
> Fat: **3 g (0 g saturated)**
> Protein: **0 g**
> Carbohydrate: **7 g**

creamy chive dressing

A healthy alternative to mayonnaise-based salad dressings.

1/2 cup low-fat cottage cheese

1 tablespoon freshly squeezed lemon juice

1/2 teaspoon Dijon mustard

1 small garlic clove, crushed

1 tablespoon snipped fresh chives

sea salt and freshly ground black pepper

SERVES 4

In a blender, puree the cottage cheese, lemon juice, mustard, and garlic. Transfer to a small bowl, then stir in the chives. Season to taste before serving.

> **NUTRITIONAL INFORMATION**
> Calories: **30**
> Fat: **2 g (0 g saturated)**
> Protein: **1.5 g**
> Carbohydrate: **1 g**

asian shrimp and green vegetable salad

6 1/2 oz. thin green beans, halved

6 1/2 oz. broccoli crowns, cut into small florets

3 oz. snow peas

7 oz. canned water chestnuts, drained

10 oz. cooked and peeled shrimp

DRESSING

2 tablespoons dark soy sauce

2 teaspoons honey

1 teaspoon sesame oil

1/2 fresh red chile, deseeded and diced

1 teaspoon grated fresh ginger

1 tablespoon rice wine vinegar or cider vinegar

SERVES 4

Bring a large saucepan of water to a boil, and fill a large bowl with ice water. Drop the green beans into the boiling water and cook for 3 minutes, then add the broccoli and snow peas. Bring back to a boil and cook for 2 minutes, then drain and refresh in the bowl of iced water.

Beat the dressing ingredients together in a large bowl, then add the drained green vegetables. Stir in the water chestnuts and serve topped with the shrimp.

NUTRITIONAL INFORMATION

Calories: 160
Fat: 2 g (0.5 g saturated)
Protein: 22 g
Carbohydrate: 146 g

tacos with beans

This is a filling and spicy lunch—keep plenty of serviettes handy!

1 red onion, sliced

1 red or yellow bell pepper, deseeded and sliced

1 teaspoon safflower oil

2 large cremini mushrooms, stemmed and thickly sliced

1 garlic clove, crushed

1 tablespoon Cajun spice mix or chili powder

2 tomatoes, chopped

14 oz. canned pinto beans, drained and rinsed

freshly squeezed juice of 1/2 lime

4 whole-wheat tortillas or chapattis (see page 44)

4 tablespoons low-fat sour cream

1 cup shredded crisp lettuce, such as iceberg

sea salt and freshly ground black pepper

SERVES 4

NUTRITIONAL INFORMATION

Calories: 230
Fat: 5 g (2 g saturated)
Protein: 12 g
Carbohydrate: 35 g

Fry the onion and peppers in the safflower oil for 3 minutes in a nonstick frying pan. Add the mushrooms, garlic, and 2 teaspoons of the Cajun spice and stir-fry for 1 minute, then mix in the tomatoes, cover the pan, and cook for 2 minutes.

Meanwhile, roughly mash the beans together with the remaining Cajun spice, the lime juice, and seasoning to taste.

Gently warm the tortillas or chapattis to refresh them and make them more flexible (see page 45), then spread each one with 1 tablespoon of sour cream. Spoon on a quarter of the mashed beans and a quarter of the vegetable mixture. Top with shredded lettuce and roll up to serve.

simple suppers

tarragon chicken casserole

This is a delicious powerfood supper packed with hunger-zapping fiber and lean protein. The garlic and leeks both contain potent antibacterial and antiviral properties, too.

4 skinless and boneless chicken thighs, about 11 oz., diced

2 large leeks, rinsed and cut into chunks

2 garlic cloves, crushed

2/3 cup chicken broth

grated zest and freshly squeezed juice of 1/2 unwaxed lemon

1 tablespoon chopped fresh tarragon, or 1 teaspoon dried tarragon

14 oz. canned Great Northern beans, drained and rinsed

6 1/2 oz. thin green beans

2 tablespoons low-fat sour cream

sea salt and freshly ground black pepper

a flameproof casserole

SERVES 4

Season the chicken and dry-fry in a nonstick frying pan for 3 minutes until browned. Transfer to the casserole. Add the leeks and garlic to the frying pan with 2 tablespoons of the broth and cook for 2 minutes, then tip into the casserole.

Pour the remaining broth into the casserole and add the lemon zest and juice, tarragon, and Great Northern beans. Bring to a simmer, cover, and cook gently for 15 minutes.

Stir in the green beans, re-cover and cook for a further 15 minutes until the beans are tender but still have some bite. Finally, marble in the sour cream just before serving.

> **NUTRITIONAL INFORMATION**
> Calories: **292**
> Fat: **4 g (1 g saturated)**
> Protein: **38 g**
> Carbohydrate: **27 g**

roasted vegetable and rice gratin

1/4 cup wild rice

1 eggplant, diced

2 zucchini, diced

1 red and 1 yellow bell pepper, deseeded and diced

1 tablespoon olive oil

2 garlic cloves, crushed

1 tablespoon chopped fresh thyme

200 g cherry tomatoes, halved

1 onion, chopped

1 1/2 cups dark soy sauce

1 1/4 cups vegetable broth

3/4 cup basmati rice

2 1/2 oz. Gorgonzola cheese, diced

2 tablespoons pine nuts

sea salt and freshly ground black pepper

a large baking sheet

a baking dish

SERVES 4

Cook the wild rice in a saucepan of lightly salted water for 35–40 minutes or until tender, then drain.

Meanwhile, toss the eggplant, zucchini, and peppers together with the olive oil, garlic, thyme, and seasoning until evenly coated in oil. Spread out on the baking sheet and roast in a preheated oven at 400°F for 25 minutes, stirring halfway through. Scatter the tomatoes over the vegetables and return to the oven for 5 minutes.

While the vegetables are roasting, put the onion in a saucepan with the soy sauce and 3 tablespoons of the broth, cover and cook for 5–6 minutes until softened. Stir in the basmati rice and the remaining broth, bring to a boil and stir once, then cover with a tight-fitting lid and reduce the heat to its lowest setting. Cook for 15 minutes, without lifting the lid.

When the wild rice and basmati rice are both cooked, mix together and tip into the baking dish. Spoon the roasted vegetables on top and scatter with the Gorgonzola cheese and pine nuts. Bake in the oven for 5 minutes until the pine nuts are toasted and the cheese is just starting to melt. Serve immediately.

NUTRITIONAL INFORMATION
Calories: 286
Fat: 9 g (3 g saturated)
Protein: 9 g
Carbohydrate: 28 g

hot and sour shrimp noodle bowl

Aromatic and spicy, this clear noodle soup stimulates all the senses. Ginger and lemongrass have traditionally been known to aid digestion and cleanse the body.

1 oz. soba noodles

1¼ cups vegetable, chicken, or fish broth

¼ fresh red chile, deseeded and sliced

1 teaspoon shredded fresh ginger

½ lemongrass stalk, lightly crushed

freshly squeezed juice of ½ lime

1 tablespoon Thai fish sauce

½ cup button mushrooms, sliced

1 tomato, cut into wedges

a handful of fresh bean sprouts, rinsed

2½ oz. cooked and peeled tiger shrimp

a few sprigs of fresh cilantro, to garnish

SERVES 1

Cook the soba noodles in a saucepan of lightly salted boiling water for 4–5 minutes or until tender, then drain.

Meanwhile, put the broth, chile, ginger, lemongrass, lime juice, and fish sauce in a separate saucepan and bring to a boil, then simmer for 2–3 minutes. Add the mushrooms and tomato wedges and cook gently for 2 minutes, then remove the lemongrass.

Put the noodles and bean sprouts in the bottom of a deep bowl and put the tiger shrimp on top. Ladle the hot soup liquor and vegetables into the bowl, and add the cilantro sprigs to garnish just before serving.

NUTRITIONAL INFORMATION
Calories: 191
Fat: 2 g (0 g saturated)
Protein: 23 g
Carbohydrate: 23 g

lamb kofta kebabs

KOFTA

14 oz. lean lamb leg steaks, diced

1 fresh green chile, deseeded and chopped

1/2 red onion, chopped

1/2 teaspoon ground cumin

1/2 teaspoon ground coriander

sea salt and freshly ground black pepper

SALAD

6 tomatoes, sliced

1/2 red onion, thinly sliced

2 heaping tablespoons chopped fresh parsley

1 teaspoon extra virgin olive oil

1 teaspoon freshly squeezed lemon juice

MINTED YOGURT DRESSING

1/2 cup low-fat plain yogurt

1 small garlic clove, crushed

1 tablespoon chopped fresh mint

8 metal kebab skewers, or wooden kebab skewers soaked in water for 10 minutes

SERVES 4

NUTRITIONAL INFORMATION
Calories: 206
Fat: 6 g (3 g saturated)
Protein: 23 g
Carbohydrate: 8 g

To make the koftas, put the lamb, chile, and onion in a food processor with the spices and seasoning. Process until finely chopped, then form into 16 small sausage shapes. Thread 2 sausages onto each skewer. Cook the koftas under a preheated broiler for 8–10 minutes, turning once or twice.

While the koftas are cooking, mix all the salad ingredients together in a bowl and divide between 4 plates. Mix the dressing ingredients together in a small bowl with some seasoning.

Serve 2 kebabs per person on the bed of salad, and drizzle with the minted yogurt dressing.

greek lemon chicken kebabs

KEBABS

6 skinless and boneless chicken thighs, about 1 lb.

1 teaspoon dried oregano

grated zest and freshly squeezed juice of 1 unwaxed lemon

1 tablespoon extra virgin olive oil

1 garlic clove, crushed

1 red onion, chopped

sea salt and freshly ground black pepper

SALAD

1/2 cucumber, diced

6 ripe tomatoes, chopped

1/2 red onion, chopped

1/2 cup mixed olives

1 teaspoon freshly squeezed lemon juice

1 teaspoon extra virgin olive oil

1 tablespoon chopped fresh mint, or 1 teaspoon dried mint

2 small heads Bibb lettuce, shredded

4 metal kebab skewers, or wooden kebab skewers soaked in water for 10 minutes

SERVES 4

Cut the chicken thighs into chunky bite-size pieces, then mix together with the oregano, lemon zest and juice, olive oil, garlic, and seasoning. Stir in the onion, cover and let marinate at room temperature for 15–30 minutes. Thread the chicken and onion onto the skewers, then grill for 10–12 minutes, turning occasionally and basting with the marinade (but do not baste for the last 5 minutes of cooking time).

Mix the salad ingredients together in a large bowl and season, then serve alongside the chicken kebabs.

NUTRITIONAL INFORMATION
Calories: **220**
Fat: **6 g (1 g saturated)**
Protein: **30 g**
Carbohydrate: **9 g**

spiced salmon with chickpea dhal

Don't be put off by the long ingredients list in this recipe; many are standard pantry ingredients and spices. The fat content may look relatively high compared to other recipes within the book, but most of the fats here are health-enhancing fish oils known to help protect against disease.

1/2 **tablespoon grated fresh ginger**

2 **tablespoons chopped fresh cilantro**

1 **teaspoon ground cumin**

1 **teaspoon ground coriander**

1 **tablespoon freshly squeezed lemon juice**

4 x **skinless salmon fillets, 4oz. each**

1 **teaspoon safflower oil**

sea salt and freshly ground black pepper

DHAL

1 **cup red lentils, rinsed**

1 **onion, finely chopped**

1 **tablespoon grated fresh ginger**

1/2 **teaspoon ground turmeric**

2 **garlic cloves, sliced**

1 **teaspoon cumin seeds**

1/2 **teaspoon black mustard seeds**

2 **teaspoons safflower oil**

14 oz. **canned chickpeas, drained and rinsed**

3 **tomatoes, deseeded and chopped**

1 1/2 **cups baby spinach, rinsed**

1 **tablespoon freshly squeezed lemon juice**

SERVES 4

Start by making the spice paste for the salmon. In a bowl, mix the ginger with the cilantro, spices, lemon juice, and seasoning, then rub into the salmon fillets. Cover and set aside at room temperature to allow the flavors to develop while making the dhal.

Put the lentils in a saucepan with the onion, ginger, turmeric, and 2 cups of water and cook, covered, for 15 minutes until the lentils start to break up.

Fry the garlic, cumin seeds, and black mustard seeds in the safflower oil in a frying pan until the garlic is golden and the seeds begin to pop. Quickly stir into the lentils, followed by the chickpeas. Simmer for 3 minutes.

Heat a nonstick frying pan and drizzle the safflower oil over the salmon fillets. Pan fry the salmon for 3 minutes on each side, until the spice crust is golden and the salmon is just cooked through, but still moist.

Stir the tomatoes, spinach, and lemon juice into the dhal until the spinach has just wilted. Add seasoning to taste, then ladle the dhal onto deep plates. Place the salmon on top of the dhal to serve.

NUTRITIONAL INFORMATION
Calories: 517
Fat: 18 g (3 g saturated)
Protein: 5 g
Carbohydrate: 45 g

mustardy mushroom stroganoff

For nights when you want dinner in a hurry, this can be on the table in just 10 minutes. Serve with basmati and wild rice or couscous, together with some green beans or cabbage.

1/2 **small onion, sliced**

2/3 **cup vegetable broth**

5 oz. mixed mushrooms, chopped if large

1 garlic clove, crushed

1 teaspoon whole-grain mustard

1/2 **teaspoon tomato paste**

1 tablespoon low-fat sour cream

chopped fresh parsley, to serve

sea salt and freshly ground black pepper

SERVES 1

Cook the onion in a covered saucepan with 3 tablespoons of the broth for about 4 minutes or until softened and the liquid has evaporated. Stir in the mushrooms, garlic, and seasoning, then add the remaining broth, mustard, and tomato paste. Cook, covered, for 2 minutes, then remove the lid and cook rapidly for 2 minutes to reduce the liquid to a syrup. Remove the pan from the heat, stir in the sour cream and parsley, and serve immediately on a bed of rice or couscous.

NUTRITIONAL INFORMATION
Calories: **108**
Fat: **3 g (1 g saturated)**
Protein: **8 g**
Carbohydrate: **8 g**

goulash meatballs

These meatballs are great to make in advance and can be frozen in individual portions. Using extra lean ground pork helps to keep the fat (especially the saturated fat) content minimal while the iron and protein remains high.

SAUCE

²/₃ **onion, very finely chopped**

1 cup chicken broth

2 garlic cloves, crushed

1 red and 1 green bell pepper, deseeded and diced

2 teaspoons paprika

14 oz. canned chopped tomatoes

1 tablespoon tomato paste

sea salt and freshly ground black pepper

MEATBALLS

¹/₃ **onion, very finely chopped**

1lb. 2 oz. extra lean pork mince

1 slice whole-grain bread, processed to crumbs

1 teaspoon paprika

1 teaspoon smoked paprika

1 teaspoon dried sage

TO SERVE

5 oz. whole-wheat spaghetti

2 cups shredded green cabbage

2 tablespoons low-fat sour cream

SERVES 6

Start the sauce by cooking the onion in ¹/₄ cup of the broth in a covered casserole for 4–5 minutes until softened. Stir in the garlic, peppers, and paprika and cook for 1 minute, then add the tomatoes, tomato paste, and the remaining broth. Season and simmer, uncovered, for 10 minutes.

While the sauce is cooking, mix the meatball ingredients together with seasoning and shape into 24 small balls. Brown the meatballs in 2 batches in a nonstick frying pan, then add to the sauce and simmer for 20 minutes.

Cook the spaghetti in a large saucepan of lightly salted boiling water for 7 minutes, then stir in the cabbage and cook for a further 5 minutes. Drain and divide the pasta and cabbage between warmed bowls. Spoon the meatballs and sauce over the pasta and top each serving with a teaspoon of sour cream.

> **NUTRITIONAL INFORMATION**
> Calories: **260**
> Fat: **5 g** (2 g saturated)
> Protein: **25 g**
> Carbohydrate: **30 g**

thai chile beef noodles

This dish has a mixture of contrasting textures in the soft noodles and crunchy vegetables, plus hot and sour flavors.

3¹/₂ oz. rice noodles

5 oz. beef rump steak, trimmed and thinly sliced

1 red onion, thinly sliced

2 garlic cloves, thinly sliced

1 fresh red chile, deseeded and thinly sliced

1 teaspoon safflower oil

1 cup fresh bean sprouts, rinsed

³/₄ cup snow peas, halved diagonally

1 tablespoon freshly squeezed lime juice

1 tablespoon Thai fish sauce

2 tablespoons chopped fresh cilantro, to serve

SERVES 2

Put the noodles in a heatproof bowl, cover with boiling water and let soak for 3 minutes. Drain and refresh with cold water, then set aside.

Toss the slices of steak together with the onion, garlic, and chile. Heat the safflower oil in a nonstick frying pan or wok over high heat. Add the beef mixture and stir-fry for 2 minutes. Mix in the bean sprouts and snow peas and cook, stirring, for 1 minute.

Stir the noodles into the pan with the lime juice and fish sauce and heat through. Pile into 2 serving bowls and serve immediately, topped with the chopped cilantro.

NUTRITIONAL INFORMATION
Calories: 349
Fat: 2 g (0 g saturated)
Protein: 14 g
Carbohydrate: 25 g

polenta pizza tart

This has all the flavor of a pizza, but with a polenta crust instead of high-GI/GL pizza dough.

PIZZA CRUST

1³/4 cups vegetable broth

1/2 cup cornmeal, preferably stone-ground

2 tablespoons finely grated Parmesan cheese

sea salt and freshly ground black pepper

PIZZA TOPPING

14 oz. canned chopped tomatoes

1 garlic clove, crushed

2 tablespoons chopped fresh basil

1 small zucchini, thinly sliced

1/2 red and 1/2 yellow pepper bell, deseeded and thinly sliced

1 cup sliced mushrooms

1/2 small red onion, thinly sliced

1 teaspoon olive oil

2 oz. reduced-fat mozzarella cheese, sliced

1¹/2 tablespoons finely grated Parmesan cheese

a few fresh basil leaves, to garnish

a tart pan, 9 inches diameter, lightly greased

SERVES 4

Bring the broth to a boil in a large saucepan. Pour in the cornmeal in a steady stream and stir until bubbling. Reduce the heat and cook for 5 minutes, stirring occasionally, until thickened. Take care to protect your hand, as the bubbling cornmeal tends to spit. Remove from the heat and stir in the Parmesan and seasoning. Pour into the prepared tart pan and let cool and firm up for 10–15 minutes.

Tip the chopped tomatoes into a saucepan, add the garlic, basil, and seasoning and simmer briskly for 10 minutes until thickened. Spread over the polenta base.

Mix the zucchini, peppers, mushrooms, and onion with the olive oil to coat, season lightly and pile on top of the crust. Bake in a preheated oven at 400°F for 10 minutes, then scatter the cheeses over the pizza tart. Return to the oven for 5 minutes, until the mozzarella starts to melt.

Scatter with basil leaves and serve cut into wedges, accompanied by a leafy salad.

NUTRITIONAL INFORMATION
Calories: 197
Fat: 6 g (2 g saturated)
Protein: 10.5 g
Carbohydrate: 26.5 g

sweet potato and haddock fishcakes

NUTRITIONAL INFORMATION
Calories: 273
Fat: 5 g (1 g saturated)
Protein: 20.5 g
Carbohydrate: 39 g

1¼ lbs. sweet potatoes, diced

8 oz. haddock fillet

3½ oz. cooked and peeled shrimp

8 cornichons, diced

2 heaping tablespoons capers, rinsed and chopped

3 tablespoons chopped fresh parsley

⅔ cup low-fat Greek (strained) yogurt

2 tablespoons cornmeal

2 teaspoons safflower oil

sea salt and freshly ground black pepper

a baking sheet, lightly greased

SERVES 4

Bring a saucepan of lightly salted water to a boil, add the sweet potatoes, cover, and cook for 8–10 minutes until soft. Drain and roughly mash in a large mixing bowl.

Meanwhile, cook the haddock in a separate saucepan of lightly salted boiling water for 5 minutes or until the fish flakes easily. Lift out of the water, remove the skin and break the fish into large flakes using 2 forks. Add the flaked haddock and the shrimp to the mashed sweet potato.

In a small bowl, mix the cornichons, capers, and parsley together. Tip half the herb and caper mixture into the fishcake mixing bowl, then stir the yogurt into the remainder to make a sauce. Season, then cover and chill in the refrigerator.

Mix the fishcake ingredients together well, adding seasoning, then shape into 8 fishcakes. If the mixture is a little sticky, use damp hands to make the job easier. Coat the fishcakes with cornmeal then chill in the refrigerator for at least 30 minutes to firm up.

Heat 1 teaspoon of the safflower oil in a nonstick frying pan and cook 4 fishcakes for 1 minute on each side until crisp and golden. Transfer to the baking sheet, then repeat with the remaining oil and fishcakes. Bake the fishcakes in a preheated oven at 350°F for 15 minutes or until thoroughly heated through.

Serve 2 fishcakes per person, with the sauce spooned over, accompanied by salad greens.

herb-crusted flounder and tomatoes

This quick and easy fish supper is full of flavor. Serve with broccoli florets and two small new potatoes per person.

2 slices seeded whole-grain bread

grated zest and freshly squeezed juice of $1/2$ unwaxed lemon

$1^1/_2$ tablespoons freshly grated Parmesan cheese

2 tablespoons chopped fresh parsley

1 tablespoon chopped fresh thyme

1 tablespoon olive oil

4 x flounder fillets, or other flat white fish fillets, such as lemon sole, $3^1/_2$ oz. each

4 ripe tomatoes, halved

sea salt and freshly ground black pepper

a baking sheet, lightly greased

SERVES 4

> **NUTRITIONAL INFORMATION**
> Calories: 175
> Fat: 5 g (1 g saturated)
> Protein: 21 g
> Carbohydrate: 10 g

Process the bread to crumbs in a food processor, then mix in the lemon zest and juice, Parmesan, and herbs. Add the olive oil to bind the mixture together slightly, and season lightly.

Lay out the flounder fillets and tomato halves (cut side up) on the baking sheet. Press the herby crumb mixture firmly onto the fish and tomatoes. Put under a preheated medium broiler and cook for about 5 minutes until the crust is golden brown and the fish is cooked through. Serve immediately.

moroccan honey and lemon chicken

Moroccan cuisine often marries sweet and savory ingredients to surprisingly good effect, as in this richly flavored sauce.

4 skinless and boneless chicken breasts, about 4 oz. each

3 tablespoons honey

2 garlic cloves, sliced

14 oz. canned chopped tomatoes

$^1/_2$ teaspoon ground cinnamon

grated zest and freshly squeezed juice of 1 unwaxed lemon

2$^1/_2$ cups bulgur wheat

$^1/_4$ cup chopped fresh parsley

2 tablespoons toasted slivered almonds, to garnish

sea salt and freshly ground black pepper

SERVES 4

NUTRITIONAL INFORMATION
Calories: **447**
Fat: **6 g (1 g saturated)**
Protein: **49 g**
Carbohydrate: **50 g**

Lightly season the chicken breasts, then heat 1 tablespoon of the honey in a nonstick frying pan. Add the chicken and the garlic and sauté the chicken breasts for 1 minute on each side over medium heat until caramelized, but watch carefully to ensure that the honey doesn't burn.

Stir the tomatoes into the pan and add the remaining honey, the cinnamon, and half the lemon zest and juice. Bring to a simmer and cook, uncovered, for 15 minutes.

Meanwhile, cook the bulgur wheat in a saucepan of lightly salted boiling water for 15 minutes or until tender. Drain well and stir the parsley and the remaining lemon zest and juice into the bulgur wheat. Serve alongside the chicken and sauce, with the toasted almonds scattered over the chicken.

chinese pork and lettuce wraps

These hand-held wraps of crisp lettuce surround an Asian ground pork filling.

1 lb. lean ground pork

a bunch of scallion, sliced

1 red bell pepper, deseeded and diced

3½ oz. mushrooms, chopped

1½ teaspoons Chinese five-spice powder

2 tablespoons soy sauce

⅔ cup chicken broth

1 carrot, coarsely grated

1½ cups fresh bean sprouts, rinsed

1 tablespoon cornstarch blended with 1 tablespoon cold water

8 large crisp lettuce leaves, such as iceberg, to serve

SERVES 4

Dry-fry the ground pork in a nonstick frying pan for 5 minutes over high heat, stirring to break up the meat. Add the scallions, red pepper, and mushrooms and cook for 2 minutes, then stir in the Chinese five-spice powder, the soy sauce, and broth. Cover and simmer gently for 15 minutes until tender.

Add the grated carrot, bean sprouts, and blended cornstarch to the ground pork and cook, stirring, until the sauce has slightly thickened.

To serve, spoon the pork mixture into the lettuce leaves (torn in half if very large), roll up around the filling, and eat with your fingers.

> **NUTRITIONAL INFORMATION**
> Calories: **407**
> Fat: **11 g (4 g saturated)**
> Protein: **25 g**
> Carbohydrate: **15 g**

pork with leeks and mushroom sauce

The satisfying savory sauce is a fabulous complement to pork.

2 x lean pork loin steaks, 4 oz. each

1/2 teaspoon olive oil

1 leek, rinsed and chopped

3 1/2 oz. mushrooms, sliced

6 tablespoons chicken broth

2 teaspoons whole-grain mustard

1 teaspoon cornstarch blended with a little cold water

2 tablespoons low-fat sour cream

sea salt and freshly ground black pepper

SERVES 2

Lightly season the pork steaks and heat the olive oil in a nonstick frying pan. Add the pork and sauté for 4 minutes on one side, then turn, scattering the leeks around the pork. Cook for 2 minutes, then stir in the mushrooms and cook for 2 minutes. Remove the pork steaks to a plate to keep warm while you finish the sauce.

Pour the broth into the pan, mix in the mustard, and boil rapidly for 3 minutes until slightly syrupy. Stir the blended cornflour into the pan and cook until the sauce has thickened slightly. Remove from the heat and stir in the sour cream. Spoon the sauce over the pork steaks and serve accompanied by roasted squash.

moussaka-filled eggplant

A healthy version of the Greek favorite, this is a good dish to prepare in advance. In addition to incorporating a host of vitamins and minerals, eggplant contains one of the most potent free-radical scavengers found in plant tissues.

2 eggplant

1 teaspoon olive oil

10 oz. lean lamb leg steaks, diced

1 onion, finely chopped

2 garlic cloves, crushed

1 teaspoon ground cinnamon

1 teaspoon dried mint

1 tablespoon tomato paste

TOPPING

²/₃ cup fat-free Greek (strained) yogurt

1 egg yolk

freshly grated nutmeg

2 tomatoes, sliced

a baking sheet

SERVES 4

Cut both eggplants in half lengthwise and scoop out the flesh with a spoon, leaving an inner shell approximately ¼ inch thick. Cut the eggplant flesh into small dice and set aside for the filling. Rub the olive oil into the eggplant shells and season the flesh lightly, then put under a preheated medium broiler for 5–6 minutes until golden brown and slightly softened. Transfer to the baking sheet.

Process the lamb in a food processor until finely chopped, then tip into a nonstick frying pan. Dry-fry with the onion and garlic over high heat for 5 minutes until browned. Mix in the eggplant flesh, cinnamon, mint, tomato paste, and 6 tablespoons of cold water, season the mixture and cook for 5 minutes.

Spoon the lamb filling into the eggplant shells. Mix the yogurt with the egg yolk, nutmeg, and seasoning, then pour this over the filling. Top with the sliced tomatoes and bake in a preheated oven at 400°F for 20 minutes. Serve with a salad.

> **NUTRITIONAL INFORMATION**
> Calories: **192**
> Fat: **6 g (2 g saturated)**
> Protein: **20 g**
> Carbohydrate: **10 g**

chickpea and vegetable bulgur pilau

1 onion, finely chopped

1 garlic clove, crushed

1²⁄₃ cups vegetable broth

1¹⁄₂ cups bulgur wheat

2 teaspoons cumin seeds

1¹⁄₂ teaspoons ground coriander

a pinch of hot chile powder

1 medium carrot, cut into ¹⁄₂-inch dice

14 oz. canned chopped tomatoes

2 small zucchini, diced

6 oz. mushrooms, chopped

14 oz. canned chickpeas, drained and rinsed

a pinch of sea salt

6 oz. baby spinach, rinsed

freshly ground black pepper

SERVES 4

Serve this Indian-style pilau with a spoonful of low-fat plain yogurt and some chopped fresh cilantro.

Put the onion and garlic in a large saucepan with ¹⁄₄ cup of the broth. Cover and cook over medium heat for 5 minutes until softened.

Stir in the bulgur wheat, spices, and carrots and cook for 1–2 minutes, stirring, then add the tomatoes, zucchini, mushrooms, chickpeas, and the remaining broth. Add the salt and some pepper. Bring to a boil, then reduce the heat, cover, and simmer for 15 minutes.

Stir the pilau, pile the spinach on top, then replace the lid and cook for a further 5 minutes. Mix the cooked spinach into the pilau and serve in warmed bowls.

> **NUTRITIONAL INFORMATION**
> Calories: 372
> Fat: 12 g (2 g saturated)
> Protein: 34 g
> Carbohydrate: 26 g

food for friends

figs with goat cheese, pecans, and honey-balsamic dressing

Figs are a great source of fiber, helping to keep you feeling full and your blood sugar stable long after you've eaten them.

2 tablespoons pecans, chopped

4 ripe figs

2 oz. goat cheese

2 tablespoons balsamic vinegar

1 tablespoon honey

1 teaspoon whole-grain mustard

2½ oz, baby spinach, rinsed

sea salt and freshly ground black pepper

a baking sheet

SERVES 4

Spread the pecans out on the baking sheet and toast under a preheated high broiler for 1–2 minutes. Watch the nuts closely to ensure sure that they don't burn. Transfer to a bowl.

Cut the figs in half through the stalk and put on the baking sheet. Cut the goat cheese into 8 pieces and put one on each fig half. Season, then put under the broiler for about 2 minutes until the cheese is golden and bubbling.

Beat the balsamic vinegar together with the honey, mustard, and seasoning to make a dressing, then divide the salad greens between 4 plates.

Place 2 fig halves on each plate, scatter the pecan nuts on top, and drizzle with the dressing. Serve immediately.

flash-fried garlic and ginger shrimp

Serve these delicious juicy shrimp spooned on a bed of tender salad greens.

1 tablespoon safflower oil

2 garlic cloves, sliced

1 tablespoon shredded fresh ginger

1 fresh green chile, deseeded and diced

8 oz. uncooked shrimp, shelled and deveined

1½ cups cherry tomatoes, quartered

2 tablespoons chopped fresh cilantro

freshly squeezed juice of ½ lime

sea salt and freshly ground black pepper

SERVES 4

NUTRITIONAL INFORMATION
Calories: 100
Fat: 3 g (0.5 g saturated)
Protein: 15 g
Carbohydrate: 2 g

Heat the safflower oil in a nonstick frying pan or wok. Add the garlic, ginger, and green chile and stir-fry for 1 minute. Tip the shrimp into the pan and stir-fry for 1 minute until they start to turn from gray to pink.

Add the tomatoes and seasoning, then stir-fry for a further 2 minutes or until the shrimp are cooked through and the tomatoes are beginning to collapse.

Remove from the heat and stir in the cilantro and lime juice. Serve immediately.

thai fishcakes with chile dipping sauce

These fragrant little fishcakes are so easy to make at home, and irresistible served with a spicy dipping sauce.

2 dried Kaffir lime leaves, optional

14 oz. haddock fillet, skinned and chopped

1 fresh red chile, deseeded and finely chopped

1/2 lemongrass stalk, finely chopped

2 tablespoons chopped fresh cilantro

grated zest from 1 unwaxed lime

1/4 cup green beans, finely sliced

a little safflower oil

sea salt and freshly ground black pepper

CHILE DIPPING SAUCE

1-inch piece carrot, very finely diced

1-inch piece cucumber, very finely diced

1 tablespoon Thai fish sauce or soy sauce

1 tablespoon freshly squeezed lime juice

1 tablespoon Thai sweet chilli sauce

SERVES 4

Put the lime leaves in a small heatproof bowl, cover with boiling water and leave to rehydrate for a few minutes, then drain and slice them thinly. Put the haddock in a food processor with three-quarters of the chile, the lemongrass, cilantro, lime zest, and lime leaves. Process until finely chopped, then stir the green beans and seasoning into the fish mixture. Using damp hands, shape into 16 flat fishcakes, cover, and chill in the refrigerator.

For the chile dipping sauce, simply mix the ingredients together with the remaining chile in a small serving bowl.

To cook the fishcakes, lightly grease a nonstick frying pan, using paper towels dipped in safflower oil. Add half the fishcakes to the frying pan and cook for 90 seconds on each side until golden brown and cooked through. Keep warm in a low oven while you cook the second batch, then serve immediately with the dipping sauce.

NUTRITIONAL INFORMATION
Calories: 87
Fat: 0.5 g (0 g saturated)
Protein: 19 g
Carbohydrate: 1 g

roasted tomato salad

Roasting tomatoes brings out their full flavor, and research shows that cooking tomatoes actually enhances their nutritional value, too, by increasing the lycopene content. Lycopene is a phytochemical that makes tomatoes red and is a powerful antioxidant.

10 ripe tomatoes

1/2 teaspoon sugar

1 tablespoon fresh thyme leaves, plus 1 teaspoon, to serve

2 tablespoons snipped fresh chives, to serve

sea salt and freshly ground black pepper

ORANGE DRESSING

1 teaspoon Dijon mustard

1 teaspoon white wine or cider vinegar

1 tablespoon extra virgin olive oil

freshly squeezed juice of 1 small orange

a baking sheet

SERVES 4

Cut the tomatoes in half through their "waists" and place on the baking sheet, cut side up. Season lightly and scatter the sugar and the tablespoon of thyme leaves over the tomatoes. Roast in a preheated oven at 400°F for 8–10 minutes until beginning to soften.

Meanwhile, in a small bowl, beat the mustard and vinegar together, then mix in the olive oil and orange juice. Add seasoning to taste.

Arrange 5 roasted tomato halves per person on a plate, drizzle the orange dressing over the tomatoes and scatter with the chives and the remaining thyme leaves. Serve warm or at room temperature.

goujons of sole with salsa verde

Salsa verde is a tangy herb sauce that makes a vibrant accompaniment to these strips of delicate fish in a crispy coating.

4 x sole or flounder fillets, skinned, about 10 oz.

1 egg yolk

⅓ cup cornmeal

grated zest from ½ unwaxed lemon

olive oil spray

sea salt and freshly ground black pepper

SALSA VERDE

1 tablespoon capers, rinsed

2 tablespoons chopped fresh parsley

1 tablespoon chopped fresh mint or tarragon

3 tablespoons chopped fresh basil

1 teaspoon Dijon mustard

1 tablespoon freshly squeezed lemon juice

1 tablespoon extra virgin olive oil

a baking sheet

SERVES 4

NUTRITIONAL INFORMATION
Calories: 155
Fat: 0.5 g (1 g saturated)
Protein: 16 g
Carbohydrate: 10.5 g

Cut each fish fillet into about 7 strips. Beat the egg yolk with seasoning in a shallow bowl. Spread the cornmeal out on a plate and mix in the lemon zest. Dip the strips of sole first in the beaten egg, then the polenta to coat. Spread out on the baking sheet, lightly mist with olive oil spray, and put under a preheated medium broiler for 5–6 minutes until crisp and lightly browned (they do not need turning during cooking).

While the goujons are cooking, make the salsa verde by blending the ingredients together with 1 tablespoon of cold water in a small food processor. Season to taste and transfer to a small bowl.

Serve the hot, crisp goujons to dip into the salsa verde.

goan shrimp curry

1 tablespoon ground coriander

1/2 tablespoon paprika

1 teaspoon ground cumin

1/2 teaspoon cayenne or hot chile powder

1/2 teaspoon ground turmeric

3 garlic cloves, crushed

2 teaspoons grated fresh ginger

8 oz. green beans, halved

1 tablespoon tamarind paste or freshly squeezed lemon juice

2 tablespoons coconut milk

14 oz. uncooked tiger shrimp, shelled and deveined

3 1/2 oz. baby spinach, rinsed

sea salt and freshly ground black pepper

SERVES 4

This quick curry will fill your kitchen with a wonderful aroma as it cooks. The list of ingredients looks long due to the many spices, but they give a complex flavor to a sauce that is made in a matter of minutes.

Mix the spices to a paste with a little water in a saucepan. Stir in the garlic, ginger, and 400 ml of cold water, add seasoning and bring to a boil. Simmer for 10 minutes until the sauce has slightly reduced and the raw flavor of the spices is released.

Meanwhile, cook the green beans in a separate saucepan of lightly salted boiling water for about 5 minutes or until tender, then drain.

Stir the tamarind paste and coconut milk into the spicy sauce base until smooth. Add the shrimp and cook for about 2 minutes or until they turn pink. Stir in the green beans and spinach and cook briefly until the spinach has wilted. Ladle the curry into bowls and serve with basmati rice or chapattis (see page 44).

> **NUTRITIONAL INFORMATION**
> Calories: 176
> Fat: 6 g (4 g saturated)
> Protein: 26 g
> Carbohydrate: 5 g

moroccan seven-vegetable tagine with quinoa

Quinoa (pronounced keen-wa) is a South American grain that has a high protein content. Feel free to vary the vegetables to suit your tastes.

2 teaspoons ground cumin

2 teaspoons ground coriander

a pinch of saffron threads

1 cinnamon stick or
1/2 teaspoon ground cinnamon

2 garlic cloves, crushed

1 tablespoon grated fresh ginger

1 onion, thinly sliced

grated zest and freshly squeezed juice of 1 unwaxed lemon

2 carrots, diced

3 1/2 oz. small turnips, halved or quartered

2 1/2 cups boiling water

15 oz. butternut squash, peeled, deseeded, and chopped

1 cup ready-to-eat dried apricots

1 eggplant, cut into 1-inch dice

1 teaspoon olive oil

2 zucchini, chopped

2 tomatoes, quartered

TO SERVE

1 1/3 cups quinoa

1 3/4 cups boiling water

a pinch of salt

a large tagine or flameproof casserole

a baking sheet

SERVES 4

NUTRITIONAL INFORMATION
Calories: 371
Fat: 2.5 g (0 g saturated)
Protein: 12 g
Carbohydrate: 80 g

Put the spices in the tagine or flameproof casserole with the garlic, ginger, onion, and lemon zest and juice. Add the carrots, turnips, and boiling water, stir well and bring to a simmer. Cover and cook for 5 minutes.

Once the tagine is underway, place the quinoa in a saucepan with the boiling water and salt. Bring to a boil, stir once, then cover, reduce the heat and cook gently for 15 minutes until the quinoa is tender and has absorbed all the liquid.

Stir the butternut squash and apricots into the tagine, re-cover the pan and cook for 10 minutes. Meanwhile, toss the eggplant with the olive oil and seasoning, spread out on the baking sheet and roast in a preheated oven at 400°F for 15 minutes until softened and golden brown.

Add the zucchini and tomatoes to the tagine, cover again and cook for a further 5 minutes. Mix the roasted eggplant into the tagine, just before serving with the cooked quinoa.

chermoula chicken with tomato pilaf

Chermoula is a fragrant North African paste that is often used as a marinade for fish, but works just as well with chicken.

Toss the diced eggplant for the pilaf with a pinch of salt and set aside in a colander for 15 minutes to draw out the excess liquid.

Lightly slash the chicken breasts so that the marinade will be able to permeate the meat. Mix the lemon zest and juice with the olive oil, cumin, paprika, garlic, parsley, cilantro, and seasoning. Rub into the chicken, cover, and set aside in the baking dish in a cool place while cooking the pilaf.

Put the tomatoes, cumin seeds, garlic, tomato paste, and 2 tablespoons of water in a large saucepan and simmer rapidly for 5–6 minutes until thick and quite dry. Stir in the rice, chickpeas, boiling water, and a pinch of salt. Bring back to a boil, stir the rice once, then cover the pan tightly and leave to simmer on the lowest heat for 20 minutes.

As soon as the rice is cooking, squeeze the liquid from the eggplant and pat dry on paper towels. Toss with the olive oil and spread out on the baking sheet. Put on the highest shelf of a preheated oven at 400°F, with the dish of chicken on the shelf below. Cook for 15–18 minutes, stirring the eggplant halfway through cooking to brown evenly.

Stir the roasted eggplant into the tomato pilaf, then serve the chermoula chicken breasts on top. Serve with a green vegetable.

NUTRITIONAL INFORMATION
Calories: 513
Fat: 8.5 g (1.5 g saturated)
Protein: 51 g
Carbohydrate: 59 g

4 x skinless and boneless chicken breasts, about 4½ oz. each

grated zest and freshly squeezed juice of 1 unwaxed lemon

1 tablespoon olive oil

1 teaspoon ground cumin

1 teaspoon paprika or smoked paprika

2 garlic cloves, crushed

2 tablespoons chopped fresh parsley

2 tablespoons chopped fresh cilantro

sea salt and freshly ground black pepper

TOMATO PILAF

1 large eggplant, cut into ½-inch dice

4 ripe tomatoes, chopped

1 teaspoon cumin seeds

2 garlic cloves, crushed

2 teaspoons tomato paste

¾ cup basmati rice

14 oz. canned chickpeas, drained and rinsed

1 cup boiling water

1 teaspoon olive oil

a baking dish

a baking sheet

SERVES 4

salmon and spring vegetable parcels

These self-contained parcels can be prepared ahead, and look most impressive when opened at the table.

4 x skinless salmon fillets, 4 oz. each

4 scallions, sliced

2 cups frozen peas

1 large zucchini

grated zest and freshly squeezed juice of 1 unwaxed lemon

sea salt and freshly ground black pepper

2 tablespoons low-fat sour cream, to serve

2 baking sheets

SERVES 4

> **NUTRITIONAL INFORMATION**
> Calories: 271
> Fat: 12 g (0 g saturated)
> Protein: 35 g
> Carbohydrate: 5 g

Cut 4 pieces of foil or baking parchment, each measuring 12 x 24 inches, and fold each one in half like a book. Put a salmon fillet on the center of one "page" and season lightly.

Mix the scallions and peas together and pile on top of the salmon. Shave the zucchini into ribbons with a vegetable peeler and divide between the parcels. Season and add half the lemon zest, then drizzle 1 tablespoon of water into each parcel. Fold the foil over twice to seal the edges, then put the parcels on the baking sheets. Bake in a preheated oven at 350°F for 10–12 minutes. The salmon will continue to cook after it is removed from the oven until the parcels are opened.

Mix the rest of the lemon zest with the sour cream and seasoning. Open up the parcels and drizzle each one with a teaspoon of lemon juice and top with a dollop of the zesty sour cream. Serve immediately.

monkfish kebabs with warm lemon dressing

20 oz. monkfish fillet

grated zest and freshly squeezed juice of 1 unwaxed lemon

sea salt and freshly ground black pepper

SPINACH

3 slices Serrano or country ham, cut into strips

2 tablespoons raisins

1 teaspoon olive oil

12 oz. baby spinach, rinsed

WARM LEMON DRESSING

3 tablespoons whole blanched hazelnuts, chopped

1 tablespoon extra virgin olive oil

1/2 teaspoon Dijon mustard

1 tablespoon freshly squeezed lemon juice

a roasting pan

4 metal kebab skewers, or wooden kebab skewers soaked in water for 10 minutes

SERVES 4

Spread the hazelnuts out in a roasting pan and toast under a preheated medium broiler for 1–2 minutes until golden, watching closely so that they don't burn. Remove any grayish membrane from the monkfish, then cut into chunky dice. Put in a non-metallic dish with the lemon zest and half the lemon juice. Add some seasoning and toss to coat, then thread onto the skewers. Cook under a broiler for 6–8 minutes, turning halfway through.

Meanwhile, for the spinach, gently fry the ham and raisins in the olive oil in a large frying pan for 1 minute. Pile in the spinach, tossing until it has wilted. Season and keep warm while you quickly make the dressing. Beat together the olive oil, mustard, lemon juice, and 1 tablespoon of water in a small saucepan. Season and warm through gently, then stir in the toasted hazelnuts. Spoon the warm dressing over the monkfish kebabs and serve with the spinach.

white wine braised halibut with crispy pancetta

2 carrots, thinly sliced

1 large leek, washed well and thinly sliced

a few sprigs of fresh thyme

¾ cup dry white wine

¾ cup fish broth or vegetable broth

3½ oz. mushrooms, sliced

4 x halibut steaks, 4 oz. each

4 thin slices pancetta

sea salt and freshly ground black pepper

a baking dish

a baking sheet

SERVES 4

Put the carrots, leek, and thyme sprigs in a saucepan with the white wine and stock. Simmer, covered, for 10 minutes, then stir in the mushrooms and cook for a further 5 minutes. Tip into the baking dish and put the halibut steaks on top. Spoon some of the liquid over the fish and season. Bake in a preheated oven at 400°F for 10 minutes or until the fish is cooked through.

Meanwhile, cook the pancetta on a baking sheet in the oven for 5 minutes or until crisp. Drain briefly on paper towels, then serve with the halibut and braised vegetables.

tuna steaks with mango and chile salsa

A fiery and fruity salsa accompanies these grilled fish steaks, and lemon-braised potatoes complete the dish.

1 teaspoon olive oil

4 x tuna steaks, 3½ oz. each

sea salt and freshly ground black pepper

SALSA

1 mango, peeled, stoned and diced

freshly squeezed juice of ½ lemon

½ fresh red chile, deseeded and finely chopped

1 scallion, finely chopped

LEMON-BRAISED POTATOES

14 oz. small new potatoes, quartered lengthways

1⅔ cups vegetable broth

grated zest and freshly squeezed juice of ½ unwaxed lemon

1 tablespoon capers, rinsed and chopped

2 tablespoons chopped fresh parsley

a ridged stove-top grill pan

SERVES 4

Put the potatoes in a saucepan with the broth and lemon zest and juice. Cover and bring to a boil, then simmer for 12–15 minutes with the lid slightly ajar until the potatoes are quite tender. Remove the lid, increase the heat, and boil rapidly for 8–10 minutes until the liquid has mostly evaporated, leaving about 2 tablespoons of syrupy juices. Stir the potatoes once or twice to prevent them sticking.

Meanwhile, mix the salsa ingredients together in a bowl and season. Cover and set aside until ready to serve.

Rub the olive oil into the tuna steaks, season lightly, then cook on a preheated ridged stove-top grill pan for about 1½ minutes on each side or until cooked to your liking.

Stir the capers and parsley into the potatoes, then spoon onto 4 plates. Place a tuna steak on top and serve with the salsa.

NUTRITIONAL INFORMATION

Calories: **231**
Fat: **3 g (0 g saturated)**
Protein: **26 g**
Carbohydrate: **25 g**

pork with caramelized apples

NUTRITIONAL INFORMATION
Calories: 248
Fat: 8 g (2 g saturated)
Protein: 22 g
Carbohydrate: 21 g

15 g polyunsaturated margarine

1 tablespoon sugar

3 eating apples, cored and each cut into 12 wedges

14 oz. lean pork fillet, cut into 1/2-inch slices

2 shallots, finely chopped

1 cup unsweetened apple juice

1 tablespoon cider vinegar

2 teaspoons cornstarch

1/2 cup low-fat sour cream

sea salt and freshly ground black pepper

SERVES 4

Heat the margarine and sugar in a nonstick frying pan until melted. Add the apple wedges and fry over high heat for 6–8 minutes until caramelized and tender, tossing the pan once or twice so that they brown evenly. Remove to a plate.

Lightly season the slices of pork, then add to the pan and cook for 1–2 minutes on each side until browned and cooked through. Transfer to the plate with the apples.

Add the shallots to the pan, pour in 1/4 cup of the apple juice and simmer for 4 minutes over medium heat until softened. Add the remaining apple juice and the vinegar, increase the heat and boil rapidly for 5 minutes until slightly reduced. Blend the cornstarch with a little cold water, then mix into the pan and cook, stirring, until thickened.

Return the pork and apples to the pan to reheat briefly. Remove the pan from the heat, stir in the sour cream, and check the seasoning. Serve with basmati rice.

glazed duck with sweet potato fries

Whereas roast duck is very high in fat, skinless duck breasts are actually very lean and have a deliciously rich flavor.

1 1/4 lb. sweet potatoes, cut into thick strips

2 teaspoons olive oil

2 teaspoons cumin seeds

4 skinless duck breasts, 4 oz. each

1 fresh red chile, deseeded and finely chopped

2 tablespoons soy sauce

2 tablespoons honey

freshly squeezed juice of 1 orange

sea salt and freshly ground black pepper

a large baking sheet

a baking dish

NUTRITIONAL INFORMATION
Calories: 358
Fat: 9 g (2.5 g saturated)
Protein: 27 g
Carbohydrate: 44 g

SERVES 4

Add the sweet potato strips to a saucepan of lightly salted boiling water and cook for 4–5 minutes until tender. Drain and toss with the olive oil, cumin seeds, and seasoning. Spread out on the baking sheet and cook in a preheated oven at 400°F for 20 minutes.

Meanwhile, dry-fry the duck breasts in a nonstick frying pan for 3 minutes on each side until browned, then transfer to a baking dish. Add the chile, soy sauce, honey, and orange juice to the frying pan, season and bring to a simmer, then pour over the duck breasts. Transfer to the oven and cook the duck and sweet potatoes for a further 10 minutes.

Remove the duck from the oven and let rest for a couple of minutes before slicing and serving with the sweet potato fries and a green vegetable or salad.

sweet things

citrus fruit salad with rose water and pistachios

This simple fruit salad makes a refreshing end to a meal and is lent a hint of the exotic by the addition of rose water.

1 pink grapefruit

1 yellow grapefruit

2 oranges

1 tablespoon rose water

1 tablespoon honey

2 tablespoons unsalted shelled pistachio nuts, chopped

SERVES 2

Using a serrated knife, take a slice off the top and bottom of each citrus fruit so that they will stand upright on your chopping board. Cut the peel away from the fruit, removing the white pith and the inner membrane. Taking each fruit in turn and holding it over a bowl, use the knife to cut down each side of the sections of membrane to remove the segments, catching the juice in the bowl. Alternatively, for a quicker preparation, peel the fruit and cut into thin slices.

Stir the rose water and honey into the citrus fruits and divide between 2 serving bowls. Scatter with the pistachio nuts before serving.

NUTRITIONAL INFORMATION

Calories: **249**
Fat: **3.5 g** (0 g saturated)
Protein: **5.5 g**
Carbohydrate: **53 g**

---

passionfruit yogurt ice

This tropical-flavored ice is a cross between a sorbet and ice cream in texture. It is fabulously refreshing on a hot day, or after a spicy meal.

¹/₂ cup granulated sugar

6 tablespoons boiling water

12 ripe passionfruit

³/₄ cup Greek (strained) yogurt

a shallow lidded freezer-proof container

SERVES 6

Dissolve the sugar in the boiling water and let cool. Cut the passionfruit in half and use a teaspoon to scoop the seeds and flesh into a sieve set over a bowl. Use a wooden spoon or a ladle to press the juice from the passionfruit, then discard the seeds.

Mix the sugar syrup and passionfruit juice together, then gradually mix into the Greek yogurt until smooth. Pour the yogurt and fruit mixture into the freezer-proof container.

Freeze the mixture for 1½ hours until beginning to freeze at the edges, then either mix well with a fork to break up the ice crystals, or tip into a bowl and break up using an electric whisk. Return to the freezer and repeat the process twice more, at roughly 1-hour intervals, then leave to freeze until firm.

The yogurt ice will freeze quite hard, so transfer to the refrigerator for 30 minutes before serving, to soften slightly. Scoop into bowls to serve.

NUTRITIONAL INFORMATION
Calories: **127**
Fat: **3 g (2 g saturated)**
Protein: **3 g**
Carbohydrate: **23 g**

cranberry and raspberry jellies

According to recent research, raspberries possess almost 50% higher antioxidant activity than strawberries and three times that of kiwi fruits.

1 tablespoon powdered gelatin or 2^1/$_4$ teaspoons Vege-gel*

2 cups cranberry juice

1^1/$_2$ tablespoons sugar

8 cloves

1 cinnamon stick

6 slices fresh ginger

1 cup fresh or frozen raspberries

SERVES 4

> **NUTRITIONAL INFORMATION**
> Calories: 119
> Fat: 0 g (0 g saturated)
> Protein: 2.5 g
> Carbohydrate: 26 g

Sprinkle the gelatin over ½ cup of the cranberry juice and set aside. Heat the remaining cranberry juice, sugar, and spices in a saucepan and bring to a boil. Simmer gently for 2–3 minutes, then remove from the heat. Stir in the gelatin mixture. Set aside to cool.

Divide the raspberries between 4 glasses and pour the cooled jelly on top. Cover with plastic wrap and chill in the refrigerator for about 3 hours or until set.

*If using Vege-gel, sprinkle the Vege-gel into ¾ cup of the cranberry juice and stir to dissolve. Simmer the remaining cranberry juice with the sugar and spices as above, then stir in the dissolved Vege-gel. Let cool and continue as above.

chocolate dipped fruits

This makes a little luscious chocolate go a long way and is perfect at the end of a special meal.

2¹/₂ oz. bittersweet chocolate (70% cocoa solids)

12 fresh strawberries

8 ready-to-eat dried apricots

8 strips dried mango

a baking sheet, lined with baking parchment

SERVES 4

Break up the chocolate and put in a heatproof bowl. Set over a saucepan of gently simmering water, making sure that the base of the bowl doesn't touch the water. Leave to melt for a couple of minutes, then remove from the heat and stir until smooth.

In turn, half-dip each fruit in the melted chocolate and put on the prepared baking sheet. Chill in the refrigerator briefly until the chocolate coating has set.

> **NUTRITIONAL INFORMATION**
> Calories: **106**
> Fat: **3 g (1.5 g saturated)**
> Protein: **1 g**
> Carbohydrate: **19 g**

spiced berry compote

This year-round dessert is made using frozen mixed berries for convenience.

2²/₃ cups frozen mixed berries

2 tablespoons sugar

a pinch of ground cinnamon or 1 cinnamon stick

2 teaspoons cornstarch or arrowroot

2¹/₂ cups low–fat Greek (strained) yogurt, to serve

SERVES 4

Put the frozen berries in a saucepan with the sugar, cinnamon, and 2 tablespoons of water. Cover and simmer for 5 minutes or until the berries have defrosted and are juicy.

Blend the cornstarch with a little cold water, then mix into the pan. Heat, stirring, until the compote has thickened. Pour into a bowl and let cool.

Serve the berry compote lightly swirled into the yogurt.

> **NUTRITIONAL INFORMATION**
> Calories: **178**
> Fat: **1.5 g (1 g saturated)**
> Protein: **8 g**
> Carbohydrate: **35 g**

white chocolate and raspberry fool

This is a pretty marbled dessert with a luxurious hint of white chocolate.

1½ oz. white chocolate

1 cup fresh raspberries

¾ cup low-fat Greek (strained) yogurt

SERVES 2

NUTRITIONAL INFORMATION
Calories: **170**
Fat: **5 g** (2 g saturated)
Protein: **10 g**
Carbohydrate: **19 g**

Chop the chocolate and put in a heatproof bowl set over a saucepan of gently simmering water until melted. Remove from the heat and let cool for a couple of minutes.

Reserve 6 raspberries to decorate, then roughly crush the remaining raspberries with a fork.

Mix the yogurt into the melted chocolate, then gently fold in the crushed raspberries to give a marbled effect. Spoon into 2 glasses and decorate with the reserved raspberries. Cover and chill in the refrigerator until ready to serve.

vanilla ricotta creams with saffron poached pears

These little set creams are similar to panna cotta, but without the high fat levels. They make a perfect foil for the tender poached pears and golden sauce.

POACHED PEARS

6 unripe pears, peeled

1³/₄ cups apple cider

¹/₄ cup honey

¹/₂ vanilla bean

a pinch of saffron threads

1 unwaxed lemon

1 tablespoon cornstarch or arrowroot

RICOTTA CREAMS

1¹/₃ cups skim milk

1 tablespoon powdered gelatin or Vege-gel*

4 tablespoons sugar

¹/₂ vanilla bean

8 oz. ricotta

¹/₃ cup low-fat plain yogurt

6 small custard cups

SERVES 6

Take a thin slice off the base of each peeled pear so that it stands upright. Put the pears in a pan with the cider, honey, vanilla bean, saffron threads, and 100 ml of water. Pare 4 strips of zest from the lemon with a vegetable peeler and drop into the pan. Squeeze the juice from the lemon and add to the pan. Cover and bring to a boil.

Simmer gently, covered, for about 40 minutes, or until the pears are tender and look slightly translucent. Turn the pears a couple of times during cooking so that they cook and color evenly, as the poaching liquor won't cover them completely.

While the pears are cooking, make the ricotta creams. Measure ¹/₄ cup of the milk into a small bowl and sprinkle over the gelatin. Set aside for 5 minutes to swell. Meanwhile, put the remaining milk in a saucepan with the sugar and vanilla bean. Slowly bring to a simmer, then remove from the heat. Stir the gelatin into the hot milk until dissolved. Let cool slightly.

In a bowl, mix the ricotta and yogurt together until smooth. Gradually blend in the flavored milk, discarding the vanilla bean. Spoon the mixture into the custard cups and let cool, then cover and chill in the refrigerator for 2–3 hours until firm to the touch.

When the pears are tender, transfer to a dish. Blend the cornstarch with a little cold water, then stir this into the poaching liquor. Heat, stirring constantly, until thickened, then pour over the pears and let cool.

To serve, turn the ricotta creams out and place each one in a shallow bowl. Serve with a poached pear, in a pool of the golden sauce.

*If using Vege-gel, sprinkle it over the cold milk in a saucepan. Add the sugar and vanilla bean and gently bring to a simmer. Let cool slightly, then beat in the ricotta, followed by the yogurt. Let cool and continue as above.

NUTRITIONAL INFORMATION
Calories: **251**
Fat: **3 g** (1.5 g saturated)
Protein: **9 g**
Carbohydrate: **31 g**

pan-fried caribbean bananas

This quick dessert is superb topped with a dollop of low-fat sour cream, and perhaps a sprinkling of pumpkin seeds. Use bananas that aren't too ripe, as they have a lower GI/GL.

2 teaspoons polyunsaturated margarine

1 tablespoon honey

2 bananas, cut into ½-inch slices

2 tablespoons golden raisins

1 tablespoon dark rum (optional)

freshly squeezed juice of 1 small orange

NUTRITIONAL INFORMATION
Calories: 264
Fat: 4 g (1 g saturated)
Protein: 2 g
Carbohydrate: 52 g

SERVES 2

Melt the margarine and honey in a nonstick frying pan over high heat. Add the bananas and sauté for 2–3 minutes until they are lightly golden and softened.

Quickly stir in the raisins, rum, and orange juice. Bubble for about 30 seconds, then spoon into bowls and serve immediately.

rhubarb and apple crumble

Oats and almonds add texture to this nutty-tasting crumble topping, and also bring the GL down.

2 cooking apples, peeled, cored, and sliced

2 cups sliced rhubarb

¼ cup honey

CRUMBLE TOPPING

2½ tablespoons polyunsaturated margarine

1 cup whole-wheat flour, preferably stone-ground

⅓ cup packed light brown sugar

⅓ cup old-fashioned rolled oats

1 tablespoon whole almonds, chopped

a 5-cup shallow baking dish

NUTRITIONAL INFORMATION
Calories: 254
Fat: 7 g (1.5 g saturated)
Protein: 4.5 g
Carbohydrate: 45 g

SERVES 6

Toss the fruit together with the honey in the baking dish. Sprinkle with ¼ cup water, then cover with foil and bake in a preheated oven at 350°F for 20 minutes.

Meanwhile, rub the margarine into the flour until the mixture resembles bread crumbs. Stir in the sugar, oats, and almonds. When the fruit is ready, scatter the crumble mix evenly on top, press down gently, then bake, uncovered, for 20 minutes until the topping is golden and the fruit juices are bubbling up around the edges.

fruit and nut bars

These chewy bars are packed with slow-energy-release ingredients. The dried fruits and nuts can be varied to suit what's in your pantry.

6½ tablespoons **polyunsaturated margarine**

⅔ **cup light corn syrup**

1¾ **cups old-fashioned rolled oats**

½ **cup ready-to-eat dried apricots, chopped**

¼ **cup dried cranberries, chopped**

2 **tablespoons sunflower seeds**

2 **tablespoons Brazil nuts, chopped**

a baking pan, 8 x 9 inches, lined with baking parchment

MAKES 20

Gently heat the margarine and corn syrup in a small saucepan until melted. Let cool slightly.

Tip ½ cup of the oats into a food processor and process until they resemble a flour-like texture—this helps the dough to hold together. In a large bowl, stir the ground and whole oats together with the apricots, cranberries, sunflower seeds, and Brazil nuts. Pour in the syrup mixture and stir well.

Press the dough into the prepared pan and bake in a preheated oven at 325°F for 20–25 minutes until golden brown and firm. Cool in the pan, then cut into squares and store in an airtight container for up to 1 week.

> **NUTRITIONAL INFORMATION**
> Calories: **126**
> Fat: **15g (2 g saturated)**
> Protein: **2.5 g**
> Carbohydrate: **15 g**

cherry and hazelnut oat cookies

These fruit and nut cookies are soft and chewy when freshly baked, then crisp up as they cool.

6½ **tablespoons honey**

2½ **tablespoons polyunsaturated margarine**

½ **cup old-fashioned rolled oats**

½ **cup plus 2 tablespoons whole-wheat flour, preferably stone-ground**

1 **teaspoon baking powder**

⅛ **teaspoon salt**

a pinch of ground cinnamon

½ **cup dried cherries**

1 **tablespoon toasted chopped hazelnuts**

a baking sheet, lightly greased

MAKES 14

NUTRITIONAL INFORMATION
Calories: **69**
Fat: **3 g (0.5 g saturated)**
Protein: **1 g**
Carbohydrate: **9 g**

Gently heat the honey and margarine together in a small saucepan until melted. Let cool slightly.

Mix the oats, flour, baking powder, cinnamon, cherries, and hazelnuts together in a bowl, then stir in the honey mixture. Spoon 14 mounds of cookie dough onto the baking sheet, then flatten with the back of a spoon.

Bake in a preheated oven at 350°F for 8–10 minutes until golden brown and firm, then transfer to a wire rack to cool. Store in an airtight container for up to 4 days.

cardamom, orange, and golden raisin pudding

This hot pudding is a cross between a bread pudding and a soufflé, with a lovely light texture. It's perfect for a chilly day.

6 cardamom pods

6 tablespoons sugar

2 eggs, separated, plus 2 extra egg whites

grated zest of $1/2$ unwaxed orange, plus freshly squeezed juice of 1 orange

1 cup Quark or farmers cheese

$1/3$ cup whole-wheat flour, preferably stone-ground

$1/2$ teaspoon baking powder

a pinch of sea salt

$1/2$ cup golden raisins

SAUCE

3 tablespoons honey

grated zest of $1/2$ unwaxed orange, plus freshly squeezed juice of 1 orange

freshly squeezed juice of $1/2$ lemon

1 generous tablespoon cornstarch or arrowroot

1 cup boiling water

a 5-cup shallow baking dish, lightly greased

a large roasting pan

SERVES 6

Sit the baking dish inside the roasting pan.

Put the cardamom pods in a mortar and crush with a pestle to extract the seeds. Discard the papery husks and grind the seeds to a powder. Tip into a mixing bowl, add the sugar, egg yolks, and orange zest, then beat for 2 minutes using an electric mixer until pale, frothy, and thickened.

Beat the Quark and orange juice into the egg mixture until smooth, then sift in the flour, baking powder, and salt. Tip in any bran left in the sieve, then stir in, followed by the golden raisins.

In a separate bowl, and using clean beaters, beat the 4 egg whites to the soft peak stage. Stir a spoonful into the batter to loosen the mixture, then carefully but quickly fold in the remainder. Pour into the prepared baking dish and put in the oven. Pour boiling water into the roasting pan to come halfway up the baking dish. Bake in a preheated oven at 350°F for 25 minutes until the pudding is golden brown and well risen.

Meanwhile, to make the sauce, put the honey, orange zest and juice, and lemon juice in a small saucepan. Blend in the cornstarch until smooth, then mix in the boiling water. Bring to a boil, stirring until thickened. Serve the hot sauce poured over each serving of pudding.

honey and lemon cake

An unadorned slice of this cake can be served with a cup of tea, but it is also great served warm, topped with a dollop of Greek yogurt, and some fresh berries or chopped fruit.

8 tablespoons honey

5 tablespoons polyunsaturated margarine

grated zest and freshly squeezed juice of 1 large unwaxed lemon

2 eggs, separated

1 cup whole-wheat flour, preferably stone-ground

2¹/₂ teaspoons baking powder

¹/₈ teaspoon sea salt

²/₃ cup low-fat Greek (strained) yogurt

³/₄ cup golden raisins

a springform cake pan, 9 inches diameter, base-lined

SERVES 10

Measure 6 tablespoons honey into a bowl and add the margarine and lemon zest. Using an electric whisk, beat for 2 minutes until pale and creamy, then beat in the egg yolks, one at a time. Sift the flour, baking powder, and salt into the bowl, tipping in any bran left in the sieve. Using a large metal spoon, fold in the flour, followed by the yogurt and golden raisins.

In a separate bowl, and using clean beaters, beat the egg whites to the soft peak stage. Stir a spoonful of beaten egg whites into the cake batter to loosen the mixture, then carefully fold in the remainder. Pour the batter into the prepared pan, then bake on the center shelf of a preheated oven at 350°F for 40–45 minutes until risen, golden brown, and firm. Cover with a sheet of foil or baking parchment halfway through cooking if the top is browning too quickly. The cake is ready when the top feels springy to the touch and a skewer inserted into the center comes out clean.

Mix the lemon juice with the remaining honey, pierce the top of the cake with the skewer, and pour the glaze all over the cake. Let cool in the pan for 15 minutes, then carefully remove and transfer to a wire rack to finish cooling. Store in an airtight container for up to 4 days. The cake is also suitable for freezing.

NUTRITIONAL INFORMATION
Calories: 194
Fat: 7 g (2 g saturated)
Protein: 4 g
Carbohydrate: 26 g

spiced apple loaf cake

This tea loaf has a lovely moist texture and keeps well in an airtight container for several days.

1³/₄ cup whole-wheat flour, preferably stone-ground

2¹/₂ teaspoons baking powder

2 teaspoons apple pie spice

¹/₈ teaspoon salt

¹/₂ cup plus 2 tablespoons turbinado sugar

3 tablespoons pumpkin seeds

1 cooking apple, cored and chopped into small dice

2 eggs, beaten

3 tablespoons safflower oil

³/₄ cup low-fat plain yogurt

skim milk (optional)

1 eating apple, halved, cored, and sliced

a 9 x 5 x 3 inch loaf pan, greased and lined

MAKES 12 SLICES

Sift the flour, baking powder, pie spice, and salt into a mixing bowl. Tip in any bran left in the sieve. Reserve 1 teaspoon of turbinado sugar for the top of the cake, then stir the remaining sugar, the pumpkin seeds, and chopped cooking apple into the flour mixture.

Beat the eggs together with the safflower oil and yogurt in a bowl, then mix into the dry ingredients thoroughly. Add a little milk if needed to give a mixture that drops easily from the spoon.

Transfer the cake mixture to the prepared loaf pan, then arrange the eating apple slices on top of the cake. Sprinkle with the reserved sugar, then bake in a preheated oven at 325°F for 50–60 minutes. Use a skewer to test when the cake is done; if any sticky mixture clings to the skewer, continue cooking the cake for a little longer before repeating the test.

Let cool in the pan for 10–15 minutes, then remove and transfer to a wire rack to finish cooling. Store in an airtight container for up to 5 days. The cake is suitable for freezing.

NUTRITIONAL INFORMATION
Calories: **173**
Fat: **5 g (0.5 g saturated)**
Protein: **5.5 g**
Carbohydrate: **28 g**

cornbread muffins

Serve these savory muffins with a bowlful of soup or a slow-cooked casserole.

1½ cups whole-wheat flour, preferably stone-ground

2 tablespoons baking powder

½ teaspoon sea salt

¾ cup cornmeal, preferably stone-ground

1 teaspoon cumin seeds

½–1 fresh red chile, deseeded and finely chopped

2 tablespoons chopped fresh cilantro

½ cup fresh or frozen corn kernels

1⅓ cups skim milk

1 egg, beaten

3 tablespoons safflower oil

freshly ground black pepper

a 12-hole nonstick muffin pan, lightly greased

MAKES 12

Sift the flour, baking powder, and salt into a mixing bowl, tipping in any bran left in the sieve. Add a grinding of black pepper, then stir in the cornmeal, cumin seeds, chile, cilantro, and corn.

Mix the milk, egg, and safflower oil together, then pour into the dry ingredients and stir together briefly until just mixed. Spoon into the prepared muffin pans, then bake in a preheated oven at 190°C (375°F) Gas 5 for 20 minutes until risen, firm, and lightly browned.

Remove the muffins from the pans and let cool slightly on a wire rack before serving.

> **NUTRITIONAL INFORMATION**
> Calories: 127
> Fat: 3 g (0.5 g saturated)
> Protein: 4 g
> Carbohydrate: 20 g

cheese and scallion whole-wheat scones

These scones make a delicious accompaniment to a bowl of soup. Whole-wheat flour helps to add fiber and lower the GL. The sunflower seeds, rich in potassium and phosphorous, protein, iron, and calcium, add a welcome crunch.

1 1/3 **cups whole-wheat flour, preferably stone-ground**

4 teaspoons baking powder

1/2 **teaspoon sea salt**

2 tablespoons polyunsaturated margarine

2 tablespoons sunflower seeds, plus 2 teaspoons for sprinkling

1/2 **cup grated reduced-fat sharp Cheddar cheese**

3 scallions, sliced

1 egg

2–3 tablespoons skim milk, plus extra for the top

freshly ground black pepper

a baking sheet, lightly greased

MAKES 8

Sift the flour, baking powder, and salt into a mixing bowl. Tip any bran left in the sieve into the bowl and add a grinding of black pepper. Rub in the margarine until the mixture resembles bread crumbs, then stir in 2 tablespoons sunflower seeds, all but 2 tablespoons of the cheese, and the scallions.

Beat the egg with 2 tablespoons of milk and stir this into the dry ingredients. Add a little extra milk if necessary to bring the mixture together to make a soft but not sticky dough.

Turn out onto a lightly floured surface and press or roll out to a thickness of 1-inch. Cut out scones using a 2 1/4-inch round cutter (re-rolling the dough as necessary). Transfer to the baking sheet and brush the scone tops with a little milk. Divide the remaining sunflower seeds and grated cheese between the tops of the scones. Bake in a preheated oven at 425°F for 15 minutes until well risen, crisp, and golden brown. Let cool slightly before serving.

NUTRITIONAL INFORMATION
Calories: 153
Fat: 5 g (1.75 g saturated)
Protein: 11 g
Carbohydrate: 15 g

index

acknowledgments

Rachael Anne Hill:

I should like to say a huge thank you to Tamsin Burnett-Hall for her fabulous recipes and to all at Ryland Peter & Small who worked so hard to produce this book.

Tamsin Burnett-Hall:

I should like to thank my mother, Diana Smith, for teaching me how to cook, instilling in me my love of food, and encouraging me to make a career from my passion.

I would also like to thank Karen Peskett for making anything and everything possible.

conversion charts

Weights and measures have been rounded up or down slightly to make measuring easier.

Volume equivalents

American	Metric	Imperial
1 teaspoon	5 ml	
1 tablespoon	15 ml	
¼ cup	60 ml	2 fl.oz.
⅓ cup	75 ml	2½ fl.oz.
½ cup	125 ml	4 fl.oz.
⅔ cup	150 ml	5 fl.oz. (¼ pint)
¾ cup	175 ml	6 fl.oz.
1 cup	250 ml	8 fl.oz.

Weight equivalents

Imperial	Metric
1 oz.	25 g
2 oz.	50 g
3 oz.	75 g
4 oz.	125 g
5 oz.	150 g
6 oz.	175 g
7 oz.	200 g
8 oz. (½ lb.)	250 g
9 oz.	275 g
10 oz.	300 g
11 oz.	325 g
12 oz.	375 g
13 oz.	400 g
14 oz.	425 g
15 oz.	475 g
16 oz. (1 lb.)	500 g
2 1b.	1 kg

Measurements

Inches	Cm
¼ inch	5 mm
½ inch	1 cm
¾ inch	1.5 cm
1 inch	2.5 cm
2 inches	5 cm
3 inches	7 cm
4 inches	10 cm
5 inches	12 cm
6 inches	15 cm
7 inches	18 cm
8 inches	20 cm
9 inches	23 cm
10 inches	25 cm
11 inches	28 cm
12 inches	30 cm

Oven temperatures

225°F	110°C	Gas ¼
250°F	120°C	Gas ½
275°F	140°C	Gas 1
300°F	150°C	Gas 2
325°F	160°C	Gas 3
350°F	180°C	Gas 4
375°F	190°C	Gas 5
400°F	200°C	Gas 6
425°F	220°C	Gas 7
450°F	230°C	Gas 8
475°F	240°C	Gas 9